The co-authors of Filled Up and Overflowing, *are both very experienced, sensitive professional organizers. Through the use of storytelling, anyone with a problem with too much clutter for too long for too many reasons will see themselves in these stories, learn the 'whys' and, most importantly, be able to make lasting changes.*

~ **Judith Kolberg**, Author, *Conquering Chronic Disorganization*, and Organizing Industry-Thought Leader

Diane Quintana and Jonda Beattie have been writing and speaking on the impact of hoarding behaviors for over a decade. They don't just write books about it, they actually live their experiences, strategies and techniques on a daily basis with their clients. One of my favorite parts of this book is their compassion for people with hoarding-like behaviors. It is easy to think that we can easily label someone as a "hoarder" and that solves their problem and yours. And, everyone who has a person in their lives with hoarding-like behaviors knows that it is not just that simple. All of the real-life stories can make the reader feel like they are not alone, and those testimonials were very encouraging to read. The book is full of applicable tips, and if the reader applies even a small fraction of the authors' strategies, they will start to see a difference in their space.

~ **Cris Sgrott**, CPO®, CPO-CD®, SMM-C

Filled Up and Overflowing *is a thoughtful, compassionate contribution to the exploration of hoarding behavior and its consequences, offering practical, useful strategies.*

~ **Alison Lush**, Master Trainer, CPO-CD®, CPO®, Certified VIRTUAL Organizer

The word hoarding alone seems to make an expert out of all who hear it, whether they are qualified or not. The unqualified people, in spite of their best intentions, may add to the misery of their loved one. With this new book on collecting and hoarding behavior, family and friends are shown what their loved ones really need: insights, compassion, and effective support. The book shows many reasons or triggers why a person might display hoarding behavior (which is not the same thing as hoarding disorder!) With respect for all the people involved, Diane Quintana and Jonda Beattie don't shy away from bold statements. They also teach soft-hearted strategies and solutions. The authors dig deeper into various backgrounds, the influence of language, developed habits, life transitions, and possible treatment and teamwork. They make this book complete by adding information about practical strategies and safety for all involved: clients, their families and friends, and professionals. Being both very experienced professional organizers, Diane and Jonda wrote another valuable view on this intriguing topic. I'm sincerely glad they did, as I am always looking for new insights and strategies to work with my type of clients. I'll gladly add this book to my prized collection of books on hoarding disorder.

~ **Hilde Verdijk**, CPO-CD®, MRPO®, Professional Organizer

Diane Quintana and Jonda Beattie's book has taken a non-clinical approach to life events, clutter, disorganization, and hoarding issues. Over recent years, these issues have often been clinically diagnosed. The impact of the media has also sensationalized a "normal" human experience [riddled with these issues] which leads to a paralysis of the individuals from dealing with them. Diane and Jonda have expertly focused their vast experience of working with individuals who present with these problems. They give the reader an understanding using everyday language without the clinical and media language and engage the reader to address them by reducing the stigma and complexity portrayed. The case vignettes throughout the book help give context, linking it to *the everyday experience. The book has a holistic approach and addresses social, environmental, and, most importantly, personal conceptualization of each individual's presentation of hoarding-like behaviors with a step-by-step plan to reduce their clutter and maintain a safe environment. The book highlights the need to have a multi-agency teamwork approach and communication, especially when there are challenges presented. There are chapters with tips for family, friends, caregivers, professionals, and a list of resources for individuals. This book will provide an alternative approach to chronic disorganization and hoarding within the normal experiences that people have.*

~ **Dr. Satwant Singh** RN MSc D.Psych, BABCP Accredited
Cognitive Behavioral Therapist, Trainer, Supervisor

Filled with tips, resources, and case studies, (and always with a client's personal and mental health in mind), Diane and Jonda tenderly and truthfully teach us about hoarding & chronic disorganization. You will feel a new sense of understanding for the person who hoards and gain new methods for working with individuals suffering from chronic disorganization.

~ **DorothyTheOrganizer**, Expert on the Emmy-
Nominated TV Show, "Hoarders"

Other Books by...

Diane N. Quintana

Now What? A Simple Organizing Guide

Jonda S. Beattie

From Vision to Victory: A Workbook for Finding a Simple Path to an Organized Home

Diane N. Quintana and Jonda S. Beattie

Suzie's Messy Room

Benji's Messy Room

Diane N. Quintana, CPO-CD® & Jonda S. Beattie, M.Ed

Filled Up
and Overflowing

what to do when life events, chronic disorganization,
or hoarding go overboard

Filled Up and Overflowing

Printed in the United States of America

First Printing, 2020

ISBN 978-1-7359684-0-7

Release Repurpose Reorganize LLC
www.releaserepurpose.com

Disclaimer
The authors have changed the names of their clients in the vignettes
and also altered and embellished the details to protect their clients'
privacy.

This book is to be used as a guide and is not intended to be used as a
diagnostic tool.

Dedication

We dedicate this book to our NAPO and ICD® colleagues who were so generous with their time and support of this project as well as the many other professionals who graciously allowed us to pick their brains.

Contents

Dr. Becky Beaton-York, Ph.D.
Licensed Psychologist

Hoarding is something that people have been fascinated by for generations. Sadly, Hoarding Disorder is one that is rarely diagnosed because people challenged by this issue rarely come forward and ask for help. Typically, the only reason they seek help is because a friend or family member reaches out for assistance.

Also, people may give someone the label of a "hoarder," because they see a filled up home or overflowing porch. However, that may not be the accurate diagnosis. Sometimes an event or different challenge in a person's life creates the illusion of Hoarding Disorder.

Filled Up and Overflowing: What to Do When Life Events, Chronic Disorganization, and Hoarding Go Overboard is the book people have been waiting for. It demystifies such events and talks about the challenges ordinary people face when tasked with reducing clutter in their homes. The authors, both professional organizers, talk to the reader as if they were right there with you, guiding you through the challenges presented in a filled up and overflowing home.

In my time working on the television show, "Hoarding: Buried Alive," I have worked with numerous professional organizers and learned multiple tips and tricks from them. Diane Quintana and Jonda Beattie are among those with whom I have worked and learned priceless strategies.

When we do therapy in an office, we focus on getting to the root of a problem and helping the client develop strategies to deal with the emotional issues. We have tried and true therapeutic methods which enable the client diagnosed with Hoarding Disorder to develop techniques other than collecting and acquiring to comfort themselves. There are times we discover the hoarding in the home is the result of an extended period of grief, Major Depressive Disorder, Social Anxiety Disorder or Attention Deficit Hyperactivity Disorder, just to name a few.

Sadly, very few therapists actually meet with clients in their home due to time constraints and logistics. Often, it is the organizers who really see what we are dealing with. Professional organizers, like Diane and Jonda, meet people where they live in their homes and see the manifestation of the problem. I can't begin to tell you how grateful I am for organizers like Diane and Jonda who understand the psychological underpinnings and know how to treat people kindly and with respect. Since they are working with the client side by side, they are not only able to provide therapists with an accurate perspective; they are able to, first and foremost, make the home safe.

In this long-awaited book, Diane and Jonda share their tips, tricks, and experiences to reduce the amount of clutter in the home. Their goal in writing this book is to give you, the reader, tools so that you can either help yourself or work with a friend or family member to compassionately unpack the environment and create a home in which you and/or they want to live.

INTRODUCTION

A drive through the neighborhood shows homes with windows covered up and junk in the yard. Does a hoarder live there? How can you know? What is the difference between collectors and pack rats? Is the person experiencing passive decline or extreme disorganization? What is going on here?

People want to know.

As a culture, we have been fascinated by hoarding since the Collyer Brothers in the early 1900s were found dead in their Harlem brownstone buried in a heap of books, newspapers, furniture, musical instruments, and rotting garbage. The New York Times in 1947 referred to them as "eccentric recluses."

Hoarding is a fascinating topic that the public is greatly interested in as demonstrated by its infusion into mainstream media.

While there is clearly a large interest and fascination surrounding the topic, the resources available don't always give the reader, movie goer, or television viewer a true understanding of what's going on. The limited way hoarding is illustrated, and further dramatized to increase viewership or sales, fosters misconceptions. Clients whose homes have been filling up for decades mistakenly think it will only take a few short weeks to restore order in their home, which is wildly untrue in clinical settings.

As we investigated the number of diagnosed (and potentially diagnosable) clients we have met over the years, as well as those who love someone with this challenge, we were left looking for a book like this one only to find that it doesn't exist.

Surveying our colleagues to get a comprehensive look of what they were encountering, we found that clients looking for help often ask questions like:

- Am I a hoarder? Is there something wrong with me?

- Why does Grandma keep so much stuff? Some of it is broken and useless. Why won't she throw it away?

- Why does Dad collect so many things? He can't possibly have room for it all.

- Is it safe to visit Mom with the grandkids? I'm worried there may be mold or things they could choke on since there's so much clutter.

- With so much stuff everywhere, where does Aunt Becky sleep?

- I'm worried that there could be a fire because of so much paper stashed in the kitchen. And if there was a fire, how would Grandma get out?

- What can I do to help? I'm really concerned about my friend or loved one.

- If Mom got hurt or had a heart attack, how would first responders get inside with a gurney? I worry about her.

In each of these scenarios, people are looking for information, techniques, and strategies to kindly, efficiently, wisely, and non-judgmentally offer help and support. Knowing how to do that is not easy. It is one of the leading reasons this book is so important.

This book bridges the gap between the educational resources about hoarding and the sensationalized portrayals of hoarding in the media. It does this through real life examples of what hoarding looks like and how it can be mitigated. Further, this book provides the reader with realistic, actionable strategies, and resources so they can tackle this debilitating disorder.

Some people's hoarding-like behavior comes from a situation. Some examples are grief (loss of a loved one or a lifestyle), depression, addictions, illness, injury, divorce, or downsizing. For instance, the client who wanted to move but couldn't face parting with anything and so couldn't downsize. Therefore, she ended up staying where she was in her cluttered home.

To help the readers, we take information about hoarding behaviors and teach the benefits of modifying some basic habits to reduce the struggles created from a hoarding lifestyle. We also illustrate the benefits of moving past the label of "hoarder" so the reader (and their loved ones) can discover new strategies to live a happier life.

Many people also harbor a fear that they are becoming affected by the Hoarding Disorder. Everyone, even the most organized among us, has some clutter in our homes. It might be the junk drawer, a spare closet, spare room, basement, or garage that has been filled with extra stuff. Some people may even wonder if this could lead them down the slippery path to hoarding. These people will also benefit from the strategies presented in this book. In an interview we did with professional organizer Cris Sgrott, founder of Organizing Maniacs, LLC in the Washington D.C. area, she stated, "We are all one nervous breakdown away from becoming a hoarder."

Filled Up and Overflowing strips away the dramatization of the Hoarding Disorder and shows it for what it really is, giving real life examples of hoarding situations and strategies used to help clients.

We share perspectives from many clients to explore hoarding from different angles. We describe what hoarding looks like and lead the reader to possible causes for extreme cluttering. The goal being that if a person can determine the reason for their behavior, then they have a much better chance of dealing with the disorder. By connecting with the stories, readers will recognize themselves or their loved ones. They will understand their plight is not hopeless and that they can utilize a variety of strategies presented to help themselves or others conquer the clutter in their homes. They will also learn the signs when the issues are greater than the family or loved ones can conquer on their own and when it's time to ask for professional help.

Our hope is that this book will generate discussions within families and can be used by professionals and others who want to assist those with hoarding-like behaviors.

CHAPTER 1

Everything You've Seen, Heard, & Read About Hoarding Is Overly Dramatized

When you see a home that is filled up and overflowing to the yard and surroundings, you think "hoarding." Hoarding is in the media quite a bit and, of course, for media to sell, drama must be presented. To even qualify for the hoarding shows, the clutter must be extreme. Usually the family is facing some dire consequences if the house is not cleared out enough to, at the very least, meet health codes. The owners of the hoarded home are put under the spotlight while up to 40 people scurry around in their space to try and meet the deadline. Naturally, there are tears and breakdowns that are captured on film. What we are seeing is the extreme. It sells television shows, but it's certainly not the norm when it comes to hoarding.

So, what exactly is hoarding?

Hoarding: Then & Now

It is a fascinating fact that long ago, pre-nineteenth century, the term 'hoard' was used to describe wealth. In prehistoric times, it was used to describe saving basic necessities. After that, the word hoarding was used to describe the protection of valuables and great wealth – a fortune – from crime. Today it is used to describe a mental health disorder. There is a growing body of literature on hoarding from the academic to the dramatic, often exaggerated, found in books, articles online, and in magazines as well as on television and in the movies. Hoarding, it seems, is everywhere.

Hoarding, it seems, is everywhere.

And with a Lifetime Television degree in hoarding, the big question or fear is, who has it? A drive through the neighborhood shows homes with windows covered up and junk overflowing into the yard. This leads to the conclusion that the person living there may suffer from a Hoarding Disorder. Some people wonder if they themselves are hoarders or if this word describes some of their family members. You probably do know someone with hoarding behaviors. But, because each person and situation is unique, it's difficult to know when the situation has crossed over into full blown hoarding.

How To Determine If You Have Hoarding Behaviors

How does one know? What is the difference between collectors, pack rats, dementia, chronic disorganization and hoarding? For those of us who work with people with hoarding tendencies, there are definitions and guidelines that we follow. The importance of using tools like this is to ensure that our opinions and feelings don't cloud a situation. By using tools, we also limit the risk of misjudging a person as being overly disorganized simply because we believe it to be so. Our list of well-vetted, industry standard tools includes the following:

The Clutter-Hoarding Scale® (a link to this document is in the Resources) developed by The Institute for Challenging Disorganization (ICD) has a list of specifications which enables the professional to assess the home as to the severity of the clutter and/or hoard. It also tells the professional how to protect themselves from being contaminated by mold, vermin, and other loose objects like exposed needles.

The Clutter Image Rating Scale (a link is in the Resources) is a series of manufactured pictures taken in several rooms of the house including the living room, bedroom, and kitchen to show the level of the clutter and/or hoard that the therapist can share with the individual. The person then rates themselves by comparing the picture to what they have in their own home.

The Clutter Quality of Life Scale, also developed by the ICD, is a multiple-choice questionnaire available to download from the ICD website (a link is in the Resources). After answering the questions, a person can see for themselves the impact clutter is having in different areas of their life: psychological distress, relationships, financial, and physical challenges. A person can then use the results of this scale to address the clutter in those areas of their life and/or home.

The Diagnostic and Statistical Manual of Mental Diseases, Fifth Edition (DSM-5) which can be used by licensed doctors and clinical therapists to diagnose Hoarding Disorder as a stand-alone mental health disease. The DSM-5 lists specific symptoms of Hoarding Disorder which you can find in the Resources.

The DSM-5 reports that 2% to 6% of the population have a diagnosed Hoarding Disorder.

As professional organizers, we cannot ethically diagnose a Hoarding Disorder, but when we see evidence that looks like it might be a hoarding situation, we do recommend the person seeks help from a counselor or doctor.

One of the first such situations was our client, Jane.

Jane's Story (Hoarding-Like Behavior)

Jane, a professional well-dressed woman, reached out to Diane because she was afraid that her heating system was going to die, and she needed help making a way for electricians to come into her home and replace the current system.

Diane went to Jane's home to conduct the interview and to assess the situation to see what help could be offered. At the time, Diane was a relatively new organizer. She rang the doorbell and from the other side she heard a voice shouting for her to come in if she could get through the door. What Diane saw when she attempted to walk in were objects stacked preventing the door from opening more than a few inches. Once through the door, Diane came face-to-face with a pile almost as high as the ceiling. She could see across the top of the pile to where Jane was on the second floor.

As Diane climbed up, she held herself in place with a hand on the ceiling and assessed the situation from there. It was hard to tell exactly where the stairs were or how Jane made her way to the second floor.

Jane's request was for Diane to clear enough of the ground floor to allow workers to come in and replace her furnace in the basement. How much work would need to be done to make that happen still wasn't clear, as Diane hadn't really made her way out of the door opening yet. As she tried to get to the same room as Jane, Diane realized that the way through was to climb the piles and swing her leg over the barely visible banister so she could hoist herself up the stairs. The banister itself was not in the best shape; duct tape was holding it together in places. The more she looked at it, Diane was fearful that it might break. When she left the assessment, she realized that this was not a job for one person and brought Jonda on as a coworker.

Jane shared that her three-level house had not always been this full of items. When her father was alive and she was taking care of him, there were open areas and the rooms could be used the way they were intended. Also, at that time she could have friends over and people could stop by and visit. But at this point, most of the rooms were filled up. Jane no longer allowed people into her home. She would meet friends elsewhere or if they were picking her up, she met them in the driveway.

At the time of the interview, Jane could sleep in her bed, use the bathroom, and do some food preparation in the kitchen, although these areas were full of clutter as well. The kitchen was also the home to two caged parakeets and two cats. Unlike the inside of the home, the outside was uncluttered; the yard was well groomed and tidy. Yet her car was stuffed full, but when asked about the items, Jane always had a good reason for the things stacked in her car. She was usually returning items or taking things somewhere and that's where they needed to be.

Jane shared that she suffered from ongoing depression and took medication. During our work together, she was friendly and talkative and had visions for how she would like her home to look one day. Downstairs (which we never saw) she wanted to turn her recreation room into a room with an animal theme. She had a half bath down there that she wanted to decorate with a Disney theme. These dreams filled her shopping lists. She continually ordered accessories for these rooms she would eventually work on. Someday.

Jane liked to dress well. She ordered clothes and a large amount of jewelry from a shopping site. She also ordered and purchased school supplies and craft items for children when items were on sale. As these things came into her home, they usually ended up in the entry hall and the room at the foot of the stairs. Most items were taken out of the shipping containers and admired; but as there was no place to put them, they were just put into stacks. We were walking on top of some of them and hoping not to break anything.

As we talked with her about a plan to make her home more into the vision she shared, it became clear that she was very fearful and worried that something of value might get tossed into the trash. Once we wanted her to throw away a box of Kleenex that was on the floor and had gotten soaked through due to a soap bottle spilling on it. She agreed, but insisted she had to pull out each individual Kleenex first to make certain nothing else had fallen into the box. When we occasionally worked on cleaning the floor itself, we would get a dustpan to sweep the little bits into and Jane would sift through these to make sure that we only discarded what she considered to be truly trash.

At first, we tried sorting the items into boxes so she could go through them after we left for the day. The thinking behind our idea was that the boxes were open. They were easy to see into and easy to sort though. But it never seemed to work. Instead, boxes were tipped over, piled into heaps and torn up. When that failed, we tried several other methods of presorting for Jane to check on later, but nothing worked. As much as Jane said she was invested in cleaning things up, she was equally derailed by the cleaning process.

So, we changed directions. Next, we looked for all of the accumulated newspapers that were more than a year old. We put them into black contractor garbage bags and labeled them for easy identification. Then we looked for old magazines and put them into big white trash bags, also labeled so she would know at a glance what was inside. Jane let us take these bags of old newspapers and magazines to a place under her deck and then cover them with a tarp so they would not get wet or be seen by the neighbors. The idea was that Jane would be able to easily access them so she could sort through the bags to recycle the stuff she no longer wanted. Of the 25 bags we stored, few if any of these newspapers and magazines ever made it to the recycling bin.

We also tried grouping like items and labeling them for easy access. We put clothes, bathroom items, kitchen items, and jewelry into bins so we could bring them closer to where they belonged. This would also allow us to begin clearing the walkways for her safety, but Jane did not want us to take the items into other parts of the house because that would cause more clutter to build in those areas.

Our stacking and sorting exercises did reveal part of the stairway, but not to the extent we wanted and certainly not wide enough for workmen to carry supplies. The sorted bags would also get reburied and sometimes chewed on (we hoped by the cats). We had to re-bag those items each time so that their messiness didn't make matters worse.

At some point, Jane turned her shopping habits towards her home and started buying accessories to help us get things organized. Our goal was to move things off the main floor so the workmen could get to the basement. Jane bought large net bags to sort children's school supplies into and another one for Disney supplies. We sorted her vast collection of Beanie Babies® into a few large plastic tubs and all were moved upstairs. She also ordered two large jewelry chests for upstairs. When everything was in its place, she seemed delighted with this result. She even ordered some shelving that she let us put together upstairs to hold cat food and litter.

Our repetitive work began to show some progress and Jane actually threw a few things away – two purses that had gotten really messy and a few shoes that were very worn, but that was all. It was concerning and discouraging.

Meanwhile, items were still being delivered to her home. We would often show up and see packages on the front steps. Knowing our limitations as organizers and the working model that healing a hoarding mindset is a team approach, we gave Jane multiple contacts for counselors and support groups. It was our opinion that these additional tools might help her unlock the barriers to moving forward. But the discussions never got very far. Once we gave her information about Shopaholics Anonymous. A few weeks later, we found the information we had given her on the floor. She picked it up, commented on it, and put it with her stack of current mail but took no further action.

There were parts of our work that Jane liked. She seemed to enjoy making lists of things to do, updating them, and crossing off completed items. Together we made posters with some affirmations and goals that served as handy reminders for Jane of the ultimate vision she had for her home. But we were all worried about the slowness of her progress and the expense. She was happy with some of the progress: the shelving, the organized jewelry boxes, the half-cleared stairs, but we felt that until she got some counseling to really investigate what was underneath her resistance to change, simply seeing the psychiatrist for medication wasn't enough. We thought we should put this project on hold until Jane was willing to do more to dig into the root issues she was up against.

After that discussion, she never contacted us again. Diane would occasionally reach out and Jane would share that she still did some of the affirmation work they had started. She would often hear Diane's advice in her mind, but the two never met in person again. Did Jane ever get her walkway cleared? Was she able to get the workmen in her basement? Did the banister ever get repaired? All good questions.

The biggest question is, of course, was this a true hoarding situation? Jane did have difficulty letting things go, even broken items. She was distressed and distrustful of others handling her possessions. She was not comfortable having anyone into her house, even though she wanted to have friends over. Her house was not safe in many areas. The banister on the stairs was loose and the pathways in the central area of the house were very narrow. There was no possible way that emergency services could get into the house, should the need arise. Nor could anyone come in to fix or replace an appliance. Many rooms could not be used as they were intended. The floor and all flat surfaces were used as storage. And Jane continued to be treated for depression, the root cause of which she never shared.

While we cannot definitively say that Jane was challenged by the Hoarding Disorder, as defined by the DSM-5, she certainly exhibited hoarding behaviors and fit many of the clinical markers of a client with a Hoarding Disorder. But is it as simple as it sounds?

Shirley's Story (Fear of Hoarding)

Diane was called by a young woman, Shirley. She was in her early thirties and concerned that she was following in her mother's footsteps. Her mother was a self-diagnosed hoarder.

When Diane went to Shirley's apartment, she noticed lots of empty boxes by the entry as well as some partially unpacked boxes. As Shirley gave Diane a tour of the apartment, Diane noticed a room on the left that was packed full. Shirley said that was going to be a guest room. The small kitchen had stuff covering all available counter space and the dining table was piled high with papers. The living room was set up nicely, but the furniture had clothes tossed here and there, books and more papers piled on the floor, and boxes in the corner. The bedroom was littered with clothes on the bed and falling out of the chest of drawers.

Diane thought to herself that Shirley might be right. Maybe she was heading towards being affected by the Hoarding Disorder.

As they worked together, Shirley told Diane that she was recently divorced, had packed up most of her belongings and moved to Atlanta to start a new job. She had not taken the time to unpack. When she started her new job, Shirley was busy figuring out how to get around Atlanta, learning her new job, and overwhelmed at the thought of unpacking and trying to organize her new home. While Shirley did not say this, Diane thought that Shirley was also likely stressed and unsettled, being newly divorced and on her own.

Working together, boxes were quickly unpacked and taken to recycling. Anything that was broken was tossed without a second thought. Clothes that Shirley thought were too small, too big, or just not what she wanted any more went into a pile for donation. Other clothes were put away.

As they worked together, Shirley revealed that she didn't know how to go about getting organized. She wasn't sure what papers to keep and how best to organize them. Shirley also wanted guidance in setting up her kitchen and pantry so that she would be able to find what she was looking for. Together Diane and Shirley created a simple filing system that she was able to follow and add to as needed. They organized the kitchen and pantry and put together the guest room.

All this work happened over the course of about six weeks. At the end of their time together, Shirley was happy and comfortable in her organized home.

Thinking back to the DSM-5, Shirley at first glance may have looked like a possible candidate for the Hoarding Disorder. Some of the rooms in her home could not be used as they were intended, and her quality of life was being negatively affected. However, once Diane and Shirley started working together, she made decisions regarding her belongings quickly. The rooms were organized, and Shirley was very comfortable and happy with the results. This seems like a case of situational disorganization. Shirley's disorganization was the result of moving from a larger home to a smaller apartment, getting divorced, and not investing time to fully acclimate to her new life.

In Conclusion

Throughout *Filled Up and Overflowing*, we will share many other stories of clients whose lives we've touched and supported. Some may look like possible hoarding situations; but as we dig deeper, you will see other problems or challenges at play. We will also share some stories where it appears at first glance like we are looking at a client who needs some help organizing; yet as we work with them over time, so much more information comes to the surface. We hear back stories, some medical diagnoses, and learn some beliefs the client has surrounding their current situation. We may feel the client does need help with a hoarding diagnosis or perhaps will benefit from receiving professional help in other areas before addressing the overabundance of "stuff" in their homes.

CHAPTER 2

Labeling and The Power of Words

What people believe about themselves and their current situation is a powerful determinant that shapes their ability to move forward or potentially freezes them in place forever. Words have power like a boomerang and can come back to taunt or haunt a person's memory long after they are spoken. In a tense situation with someone experiencing hoarding-like behaviors, it's easy to throw around labels, jargon, and other such words to clarify both what is going on as well as to sum up the experience. But make no mistake that words like "hoarder," "packrat," and "slob" carry a big message that can cause more harm than good.

When speaking about hoarding, we truly want you to exercise caution. Be careful with how you speak about the person and their hoarding behavior. Mind your words so that you don't close doors you're hoping to open or worse, push someone away out of shame, embarrassment, or ridicule. For most people, hearing from a loved one or caregiver the label of "hoarder" is not a new thing; they have likely called themselves these names for a long time. But it's like a betrayal when someone in the role of helper/ supporter turns from being a voice of reason into a voice that mirrors their own internal dialogue.

Be kind. Be considerate. Be aware.

Here is where you need to start.

Understand the Role Labels Play in Your Life

As professional organizers, we're very familiar with labels and they are wonderful when applied appropriately. For example, it's so much easier to find a file you're looking for when it's labeled appropriately. Countless hours have been lost searching for documents not placed in the right file. Had it been inside a file with the correct label on it, it would have been easy to spot! Labels allow you to jog your memory. You know what's inside the container: box, basket, tub – when it is labeled with the contents. People even label shelves in closets or garages to help identify the correct space to return items. The practice of labeling not only makes it easier to find things, but it reminds us where things go after using them.

Labels work best when they have a real meaning for the person using them. Jonda, for example, would probably place her mammogram results in a file with the doctor's name in it. A client she worked with placed it in a file labeled "boobs" believing that the doctor's name was less memorable than the area of her body being examined. There is no true right or wrong way to file things; it just needs to be useful to the person using the files.

Labels for People

Historically, labels were used for much more than identifying papers and things. They are also used to help identify what a person did for a living. According to Wikipedia, a person's surname served a community purpose for several centuries. In the middle 1400s, Mr. Baker was probably the town baker. Mr. Smith was most likely the town's blacksmith. Mr. Miller probably ran the mill. In this way, labels act as shortcuts, giving people credibility and an easy way to access their value in a community.

Be kind. Be considerate. Be aware.

Surnames have most often been used to collect people together. Clans all used the same surnames. For some, the use of a surname was a source of safety, for others pride. As communities moved into more of an individuated society, surnames lost their ability to define a person, but the need for shortcuts to help explain someone has not been lost but merely made more complex.

Today, we use many different labels to explain a person, but the words carry less clarity and require more discussion to really get underneath their meaning. For example, being introduced to Diane as a co-author of this book, you would also likely learn that Diane is more than just a writer. She's also a wife, mother,

gardener, public speaker, dancer, and a teacher. When we introduce two people together, often we use these additional labels to
help increase camaraderie between people. "Diane, I'd like you
to meet Jodi. She is also a great gardener." When you introduce
people to each other in this way, it provides an instant connection. The two people know they have something in common.

Labels are also helpful when talking about bigger issues like
mental health challenges or diagnoses. On the positive side, labels
help mental health professionals identify the most effective form
of treatment for an illness. These professionals can look back at
years of research about similar symptoms with other people who
have experienced this illness and see what treatments were the
most beneficial.

Labels in this way carry a great social value. They continually
offer shortcuts so people know more about a person or a situation. The challenge with labels is in these same shortcuts. On
one hand, descriptors like "gardener" provide you with a base
of understanding, but they only go so far. When you use more
charged words like "messy" or "hoarder," they imply details
around those words that can be fraught with misconceptions,
false assumptions, and even outright lies.

Labels can be cruel and never tell the whole story. They are useful
to describe a diagnosis, but they leave out the human inside of
the story. They don't define a person but merely give information about one small characteristic and leave you with a list of
assumptions about what the label means.

In many cases, we are dependent on labels to get the ball rolling. Medical offices require codes and diagnosis to offer services. Schools require the same for kids who receive special accommodations ranging from free lunch to time with the guidance counselor. Pharmacies and insurance companies require labels to know what services can be paid for, what copays are due, and what medicine can be distributed.

Underneath this is the need to call circumstances by a particular name and those names carry weight and meaning with them. That said, there are consequences for the human underneath the label as Jonda found out with her class.

Several years ago, Jonda worked as a special education teacher and she did a little experiment with her class. She brought three outfits into her classroom and hung them on hooks at the front of the room. One outfit consisted of scruffy tennis shoes, old, stained jeans, and a stained t-shirt with a small hole on the sleeve. The second outfit was a tailored suit with a ruffled blouse and polished black pumps. The third outfit was a beautiful ball gown with matching dance shoes. The children were to study the outfits for a while and then share who they thought those clothes might belong to.

The children described the person who would belong to the first outfit with words like poor, homeless, sloppy, smelly, and stupid.

They chose words like smart, professional, lawyer or banker, and neat for the second outfit.

For the last outfit they chose words like beautiful, princess, wealthy, or model.

There was more conversation, of course, and the children made up stories about the people they imagined wearing these clothes. They decided what work they might do, where they might live, and what their lives were like. The clothes triggered labels that expanded the musing about what kind of life or life circumstances the person wearing the clothes was living. Without much direction, the children easily jumped to conclusions as they heard their fellow classmates talking. It was a great exploration into their imagination and how something as small as clothing can lead to such great deductions, even in the absence of actual facts, data, or input from the teacher.

The energy was high, and the kids had fun with this exercise. But you can imagine that the room got a bit quiet when they were told that all three outfits came from their teacher's closet. The first outfit was used for work around the house like gardening or painting the deck. The second outfit was for giving presentations or going to church, and the third outfit was worn during ballroom dance competitions.

Each one fit the teacher, someone who was not poor or a model, but merely a hard worker who had different facets to her life. The lesson for the kids was a great example to "not judge a book by its cover" and of course, this is the danger of labels. The clothing a person wears is a reflection of what they are doing in the moment, not who they are as a whole. You can only speculate, as the children did, about the story underneath if you don't take the critical step to ask questions.

In our society, people jump to conclusions when the only information they have is what they see. If you see a dumpster outside someone's house, you assume (often correctly) that the family is removing junk or trash, perhaps remodeling, or preparing their home for sale. The clients we work with often carry a deeper shame about removing items from their homes. The fear of the "neighbor noticing" and judging them can be so powerful that they refuse to tackle the work at all. It's easier to live in the very full home than it is to risk being "seen" or judged as a hoarder.

When we work with clients, it is important to know what their deeper concerns are. We ask about their history, how they have managed organizing their home in the past, and if they have a vision for the end result of the organizing project. One client worked hard to convince her mother to get help clearing out her small home before moving into an assisted living community near her daughter. Her daughter contacted a "clean-out" service to come and give an estimate, but when the company rep showed up, he took a walk through and then said, "Well, it will take at least three dumpsters."

While he may have been factually accurate, his comment was so insensitive that the client thought he was actually going to put all of her belongings into a dumpster. She felt the shame of his judgment and as if he were calling her belongings "junk." His lack of care and consideration caused her to say no to the whole endeavor. All of her daughter's work to help her get into a safer, cleaner home was lost because of this one little sentence.

That's how judgment works. It cuts to the quick. It speaks directly to a person's deepest insecurities. And, when that person is vulnerable, labels and assumptions can disintegrate progress. In this case, it was a long time before the daughter could get her mother to agree once again to explore downsizing. This time, a professional organizer was called in and the story was shared *before* meeting with the mother. This allowed the organizer to show greater empathy and care to everyone involved. She took the time needed to earn the trust and respect of the family before successfully completing the job.

Labels are helpful in many ways. But mislabeling, not knowing what or how to label things and people with sensitivity, kindness, and accuracy, can cause more harm than good. That said, labeling challenges are not just limited to people. When you don't know how to sort, separate, or categorize items, it's hard to move forward as well. This was the case with Diane's client, George.

George's Story (Categorizing Skills)

George called Diane to help him clear out his apartment. The apartment complex wanted to renovate, and they gave him six months to empty his unit. He had the option to move within the complex or move on to a different location.

At first glance, the apartment was full of all manner of things. George had boxes and boxes piled about. Some boxes had their contents spilling out. Diane could see glass, books, magazines, CDs, cassette tapes, Styrofoam, and papers all jumbled together. It looked like a very full hoarded home, except that these things were fairly tidily put together. There was very little debris or trash on the floor. No doorways were blocked. Passageways were clear and able to be walked through. There were no fire hazards or concerns from a public health perspective.

Yet at the same time, it was full of stuff.

In contrast to the sense of fullness Diane felt walking in, it was also clear that somehow George was making this home work for him. There was a portion of the couch that was clear and empty. This was where George sat to eat his meals and to watch TV. There was also a portion of his twin-size bed that was also clear, making room for George to sleep. Where George needed to make room for himself, it was neat and clean. So why the discrepancy with the rest of the house? When George and Diane finally talked, he shared that while he hated living this way, he felt stuck – trapped with all the stuff he had and didn't know what to do with. George didn't know what to keep and how to keep it. Organization confused him and tasks like "what could be recycled" or "what needed to be thrown away" stopped him cold. George wanted to do the right thing, but the decision-making left him feeling trapped among the boxes.

Diane started simply. She asked about the papers. Where did they come from? What purpose did they serve to George? What meaning was behind them all? And of course, yet to be asked was, "what could he let go of to make room for himself among all the stuff?"

It turned out that George had taken over his elderly mother's paperwork, including her finances and monthly bills since his father had died. He was also the executor of his father's estate which left him feeling an obligation to not make any mistakes with his mother's security. This mix of responsibility meets fear left him feeling paralyzed. George had no clue what was important to keep and what could be shredded.

This is where Diane got to work.

It's important to note that as organizers, we never make definitive rules about what to trash, shred, or file. Our rule is to ask clients to check with their accountant about important documents so questions around how long to keep things, and in what format, are answered by the professionals with the greatest knowledge. Diane had George check with his accountant and make a list of what to keep and how long to keep it. Then, they worked together to create a filing system that was easy to access and had simple labels so George would know what stuff was, where it belonged, and how to find things when he needed it. Once they had the system in place, it took them no time at all to fill the folders and determine which remaining papers were to be shredded or recycled.

Once the papers were managed, they explored the rest of the apartment. Diane worked with George on making easy decisions first. He began with his books, magazines, CDs, and cassette tapes. As he had collected these items for years, they were mixed together in piles all over his home. One area that is often accessible to clients is around "usability," so Diane asked George how he utilized these different items. He admitted that for a good period of time, he has listened to his music through one of the apps on his phone. In his words, rarely would he ever put a CD or cassette tape into his music player anymore to hear it. The app gave him easy access to all the music he loved and the convenience of it had already proven useful in his life. In fact, it was his preferred way to listen to music.

By exploring the concept that he wasn't losing his music but rather looking at "how" he was able to access it in the future, this released George from the need to "hold on" to the actual CD or tape. He realized that he wasn't losing anything by letting go of the physical items. What he gained by doing so was the space he deeply desired in his apartment. Once he said out loud that he really didn't feel a need for the items, it became easier for him to put CDs and tapes into boxes to donate.

Next, they tackled the books.

Diane told him that the VA Hospital loved to have books and magazines for the patients to read. It turned out that George's father was a military man. Giving back in this way aligned with one of his core values and he became like a man on a mission. He put together a big stack of books to donate there. The remaining books George packed up, ready to move.

What became clear as they worked together was that George didn't like the idea of just throwing things away. If there was another use, another person who would benefit from the item, that was his preference. So, Diane taught George about the local Atlanta recycling center. They researched what was recyclable so he had a clear picture of what could be donated there versus the traditional garbage. After this, George began working his way through items that could be taken to the recycling center. Little by little, he worked his way through all of the piles, clearing out what could be recycled, donated, or trashed. Soon the only things remaining were the pieces of furniture and belongings that George was going to take with him when he moved.

What happened to George is not all that uncommon. He had become stuck – essentially paralyzed – because he didn't know how to decide what to keep and what to get rid of. His desire to protect his mother from harm caused him to store years of useless papers simply because he didn't want to be caught unaware. His love of music caused him to keep all of the different ways it could be played because he didn't want to be without this joy in his life. Yet he had moved away from these items long ago and didn't see it.

Labels work when they are used with care.

Because he didn't know how to think through what to keep and what to let go of, he did nothing. His story is all too common for folks in these kinds of situations. And for many like George, the piles grow to the point where it was too overwhelming to do alone. But once the questions are asked, it becomes easier. Releasing extra stuff for the good of one's mental and emotional health is much easier with an extra set of hands. George couldn't do this alone; but with Diane's help, he was able to clear his home and move on.

Labels work when they are used with care – when they help clients see things clearly or help organize items in a way that makes them easier to find when needed.

But labels are not just words on the side of a box. Just as the wrong words on a box can cause disorganization, frustration and angst, the wrong words said inside one's mind can do even more harm.

Perhaps the most destructive use of labels are the ones we say to ourselves about ourselves.

Self-Labeling

We all do this. Something happens and we make a wrong turn or we say the wrong words and inside the quiet of our own thoughts, we utter things like, "how could you do that?" or "what an idiot" or some other self-reprisal meant to clue you in to the error of your ways. This is self-labeling, and it's delivered to you via your inner monologue. This internal self-talk is incredibly powerful. An article in the Journal of Personality and Social Psychology (the link is in the References) shows that the words we use to describe ourselves as well as how we address ourselves (in the first person or more removed as if we're talking about ourselves) make us more or less vulnerable to stress, anxiety, and sadness.

You can imagine that an inner monologue that includes words like "lazy," "stupid," "messy" or "loser" translates into a self-perception that's negative. The labels we use can be downright toxic and harmful. Labels like this are also overly simplistic and rarely capture the complete picture of what's going on.

For example, when a person calls themselves "lazy," this label may describe a specific action, or it could be a label they have lived with their whole lives, given to them growing up. Is laziness real or is it a disguise for something deeper? Perhaps accomplishing tasks are harder for them because they have a learning disability or ADHD and struggle to focus? Maybe their "laziness" is because of an underlying depression or life challenge that causes their mood and motivation to drop? Is the label of "lazy" a cover up for what is really going on? Or is it something they were called so often as a child/young adult that they now believe it?

"Stupid" or "slow" is another label that can be deeply harmful. People may use this term when they make a mistake or have a tough time learning a new skill. Sometimes it's used because a person has a set of standards that they can't meet. The internal monologue isn't comparing their efforts to others but rather to their own expectations. When a person uses negative labels in this way, they defeat themselves before they've even begun. The label acts as a forgone conclusion, often causing people to give up on a new task before they even get started.

As professional organizers, we often get calls from people about what they call a "hoarding situation." Sometimes it is the individual themselves calling to say they are a "hoarder." Other times, it is a concerned family member seeking help for their loved one to make their home safe and livable. In both instances, a self-diagnosed "hoarding" problem has been declared often without a professional or proper medical diagnosis.

This isn't to say that the concerned person shouldn't raise their concerns, quite the contrary. It is to say that when these concerns are raised, it's important to address what is seen and factually clarify before declaring someone to be a hoarder. The label alone conjures up visions from mainstream media of dark, squalid, filthy, trash-filled environments. Creatively, people think of hoarders as the dramatic depiction seen on TV and in most cases, this is simply untrue.

Remember that according to the American Psychiatric Association (a link is in the References), only 2-6% of the population have a true hoarding diagnosis. Everything else is "hoarding-like" behaviors with a lesser degree of severity and complexity which often can be resolved with the right support. The best way to take loving action is to ask and minimize the use of labels without a professional diagnosis. This is the kindest way you and your loved ones can move forward.

Here's What We Learned While Working with Grace

Several years ago, Jonda worked with a client who was diagnosed with severe ADHD and depression. Both labels were given to her by a medical professional and she took medication to help when she could afford it. This meant the help she received was sporadic. At times, she managed her emotions on her own and over the years had developed "skills" to move her life along. While she was OK with the labels because they helped her get professional/ medical help, because the help wasn't consistent, she also struggled a lot.

For example, Grace would get very frustrated when working on projects that required a lot of concentration. When things didn't go smoothly, she would repeatedly shout out, "Stupid, stupid,

stupid! This is not rocket science. I should be able to do this."
Her outbursts released some of her frustration, but it didn't help
her self-confidence. Grace and Jonda talked many times about
the simple fact that she was in no way "stupid." She was, in
fact, gifted in many areas of her life. To turn this around, Grace
needed to stop being so mean to herself when things didn't come
easily. Her underlying challenges were in fact very real. Patience
and kindness were the keys to helping her make greater progress.
As Grace learned the deeper implication of her self-talk, she came
up with a new phrase and asked Jonda's permission to use it when
they worked together. Now, instead of yelling "stupid" when she
made a mistake, she said, *"F..k, F..k F..k! This is hard but I will
get it."* The absurdity of her words would make them both laugh
and release some tension, allowing her to take a much-needed
deep breath and try again.

Sometimes, Labels Are Less Overt

Diane's client, Ginger has a beautifully organized home with the
exception of two rooms: her office and a downstairs craft room.
Ginger has many hobbies (certainly more than the average person)
and tends to try to work on them all at the same time. This leads
to piles of papers, books, and crafts scattered between the two
spaces with projects in various stages of completion. Each one
stopped at a particular moment and left to be picked up when the
inspiration hit her. Rarely does Ginger finish these tasks on her
own. When she has assistance, things can move along, but on her
own, Ginger's crafts are incomplete at best.

When she started working with Diane, it became clear that Ginger
really did accomplish a lot when she put her mind to it. Working

together, Diane and Ginger made measurable progress in a very short period of time. So, the question remained, why can't Ginger do the same on her own?

"What's wrong with me?" She would ask. "Why can't I do this without you? Is there something wrong with my brain that I can't seem to move ahead without you?" Ginger's frustration grew as she continued to work with Diane, each completed project leaving her feeling confused about what stood in her way.

Part of the support Diane offered Ginger was missed in her assessment of the situation. It's not that Ginger was incapable of doing things on her own. The problem was on her own, the steps forward were often unclear. Making decisions about what to do next confused her. Because of this, she allowed her mind and behavior to quickly wander to something new that caused her less stress.

She was also quite guilty of some seriously negative self-talk. Ginger repeatedly labeled herself stupid and lazy because of her inefficiency finishing tasks without help. Her belief that she was a failure came through at her most vulnerable times and because of this, it sunk in deeply. Ginger believed these things to be true and Diane recognized that her real block was her self-talk. But, because self-talk is such a solo activity, Diane needed to raise Ginger's awareness. For Ginger to change, she first had to become aware of how often and in what ways she beat herself up with her words. To do this, she suggested Ginger keep a running list of her ideas as they occur to her. This caused Ginger to see for the first time how deeply she sabotaged herself and her efforts.

In Conclusion

Labels when used appropriately serve a vital function. They identify people, places and things, making life much easier for all of us. When negative labels are applied, they can be hurtful, demeaning, and cause stress. We believe that the negative connotation implied by the label 'hoarder' is so strong that people should think twice before assigning that label to someone or themselves. After all, we know the person is so much more than their hoard. Negative labels wound us in ways more severe than a physical wound. A cut on our body will heal over time. We may be left with a scar to remind us of the wound but, unless it is life threatening, this type of wound will heal. Words are often repeated in our minds. Once someone, including ourselves, gives us a label, this is how we refer to ourselves over and over again until this is the only way we think of ourselves. We don't think of the other words which may describe our many other positive characteristics; we only remember and repeat the negative one. We urge everyone to keep this in mind before assigning an unhelpful negative label to someone.

CHAPTER 3

If Not Hoarding, Then What?

As professional organizers, our relationship with clients begins when they reach out. There is very little outreach done from our end. We really come into a person's life when they (or someone they love) decides it's time to seek out help. When this happens, one of our first steps is to conduct an assessment to determine the level of a person's disorganization and how long they have been challenged with organization in their lives. It's at this point that many clients self-identify as having a Hoarding Disorder. As we listen to their stories, we often wonder if it's really hoarding or could the overwhelming disorganization be the result of something else? Very often, that is the case.

In this chapter, we define some of the most common disorders we have seen co-exist with traditional hoarding. We also share some of our client's stories (their names have been changed to protect their privacy) to help explore how life experiences can mimic true hoarding when in fact, the disorganization really is a result of some other life event or experience. Each vignette allows the reader to find themselves in the stories and see that there is hope for their personal situation.

If your role is to support someone who self-identifies as having a Hoarding Disorder, this chapter will help you gain a better understanding of the true nature of the disorganization and some examples of how we worked with clients to help manage the issues. If you are someone who personally self-identifies as having a Hoarding Disorder, we offer this section for you to consider and reflect on what might be going on for you at a deeper level. Not all people who have large collections, or even those who are chronically messy, are affected by the Hoarding Disorder. It's important to not only know the difference, but to talk to yourself in ways that don't overly dramatize or inflate the situation you're living in.

Self-Diagnosis

Our first glimpse that a person may self-identify as having a Hoarding Disorder comes during our intake call. It's at this time that a client may tell us that they are a hoarder or that they have experienced hoarding in the past. We always take this "self-imposed" label to heart. It gives us a picture of how they see their lives and how overwhelmed they feel about the challenges they're facing. Given that we are not psychologists or medically trained doctors, we do not diagnose the client's behavior. But we do take their self-assessment as a signal to watch in case a referral to a mental health professional is needed. As we start working, we often discover that the Hoarding Disorder behaviors may well have roots in what appears to be a different disorder. Finding out more about what might be triggering the hoarding-like behaviors can often lead the client to seek professional help. We always support this endeavor because if the source of the behaviors can be treated, decluttering the home may progress more easily.

Common Disorders That Can Intensify Hoarding Behaviors

We all have reasons for hanging on to things that are not needed or sometimes not even wanted (think grandmother's huge armoire). Some people keep items and then in due time, make peace with letting go of the item and do so. Other people have disorders that make it even more difficult to get rid of *any* item. When that happens, collections overflow into living spaces, making rooms uninhabitable. It's important to note that for many people their attachment to "things" is temporary. That is not uncommon. It's when someone chronically collects, refuses, or is unwilling or unable to let go, despite the health or wellness implications. That is when we are called in.

Here are some common disorders that operate alongside or are often diagnosed as the root issue when a client self-identifies as a hoarder. Included are vignettes to illustrate the strategies and solutions that help our clients move through challenges like this in their life.

Chronic Disorganization

Chronic Disorganization is not a medical disorder but more of a behavioral pattern. It is a history of disorganization where efforts to get organized cannot be maintained and there is an expectation by the person that they will continue to be disorganized.

Additionally, the disorganization affects their quality of life on a daily basis. They may even feel emotionally traumatized by their clutter. They feel overwhelmed and helpless. When people affected by chronic disorganization receive professional organizing help to teach them skills, they develop their own unique approach to organizing. In most cases, the hoarding-like behaviors reduce and the symptoms drastically lessen.

Winifred's Story

It took several years for Winifred to call Diane because of her overwhelming shame that her small apartment was in such a disastrous state. As she explained over the phone, she was very anxious. The amount of clutter in her home was very stressful to her. She constantly worried about being late to work, paying her bills on time, doing her laundry, losing her keys, and misplacing important paperwork among other things. Diane listened as Winifred described her living situation, her feelings, and her problems. Then, she got right to the heart of the matter by asking Winifred the core question: What is bothering you the most right now? Winifred told her that she had a new boyfriend who she wanted to invite over, but she couldn't. She was afraid she would never see him again if he saw the inside of her apartment. She couldn't risk that.

Ultimately, Winifred was tired of coming up with excuses for why he couldn't set foot inside her home. If she could just clear out the living room to begin with, she could at least invite this guy through the front door. Winifred knew she had to overcome her anxiety and ask for Diane's help.

During Diane's first visit, she and Winifred tackled the entry, the tiny kitchen and the dining area which was to the left of the front door. They worked for about four hours and cleared the kitchen floor which was covered by empty boxes, 12 packs of soda, full garbage bags, and packing material from the empty boxes.

As they worked, they talked. Diane found out that Winifred worked long hours and didn't have a routine for tackling the mail or for putting away groceries. Her habit was to open the package and toss the packing on the ground along with the empty box. The contents of the boxes were often clothes which were tossed into the dining area or books which were placed on a side table in the living room. Winifred told Diane that opening mail made her anxious because she was afraid of throwing something important away by mistake. Her routine was to just pile it on the dining table and let it sit until she had enough time to deal with it. The problem was that she never wanted to deal with it.

Towards the end of this initial visit, Diane sat with Winifred to review what they had done together and to create a plan. They decided to work together every other week for four hours at a time. On the weeks when they didn't work together, Winifred would concentrate her efforts on maintaining the organization thus far and on creating one new habit.

The first habit was for Winifred to deal with the mail. She had to decide what was recycling, what was shredding and what needed follow up. The next step was to schedule time to follow up by either making a call, writing an email, or paying a bill. If a package arrived, Winifred's new habit to build was to toss the packing material, recycle the box, and put the contents of the box where it belonged. If it was clothes, they went into a drawer or the closet. If it was a book, it went on the bookshelf until Winifred was ready to read it.

It took time, months in fact. Winifred understood that the apartment didn't become that messy and cluttered overnight, so it was not going to become organized overnight. She also realized that it was important for her to learn how to organize and to build new habits for dealing with mail, her groceries, her clothes and laundry, as well as some basic cleaning strategies. At the end of their regularly scheduled twice-a-month organizing sessions, Winifred was happy. She was no longer anxious and stressed. Her home was organized and mostly clutter free. She could find her keys. Getting dressed for work was a snap. She had a routine for taking care of the laundry and she knew exactly where her important papers were filed. Best of all, she felt comfortable opening her door and inviting her boyfriend over. She had let him know that she was working on getting organized and wanted him to see the apartment at its best. It turns out that his apartment was somewhat disorganized, so he understood and patiently waited for his invitation.

Diane still works with Winifred about twice a year to tweak the organizational systems and to provide support. We share these strategies in greater detail in Chapter 6, Reducing the Clutter.

It's important to note that organizing, no matter how organized a person you are, is not a once and done task. Every now and then things get a little messy. When that happens, you deal with it.

Situational Hoarding

Situational Hoarding is also not a medical disorder. It is generally triggered by a life event. Everyone has big life events in their lives but sometimes these events drown us. We experience a huge loss; someone we love dies or divorces us. Perhaps we were downsized at work or have lost our job entirely. We may even seek to ease the pain created from this loss by overshopping or collecting. Conversely, we may be promoted and find that the new job takes all our time and energy. There might be a new baby that adds extra work to our already full schedule. These are events which happen to lots of people. The difference here is that someone affected by situational disorganization does not get out from under the life event and their personal space reflects the stress, chaos, and clutter they feel inside.

Perhaps a person was raised in an environment where life skills were not taught because everything was done for them. Now they are living on their own and don't have a clue. Life changes that make organizing suddenly more complex can result in overwhelm which results in hoarding-like behaviors. Once people understand what the root of their problem is, they can move forward and, with help, improve their situation.

Bridget's Story

Bridget was by nature a very organized person. She had taught first grade for a number of years before deciding to be a stay-at-home mom. When she was working at school, she had successfully managed her classroom, taken care of her housework, done the bill paying, filed her papers, and cooked dinner several nights a week for herself and her husband. When Bridget found out she was pregnant, she had visions of baking cookies with her children, playing educational games with them, hosting playdates with other children and their mothers, and keeping a beautifully organized home. In essence, being the perfect mother and wife.

All these visions went straight out the window when she brought the twins home from the hospital. At first, things were fine. Bridget's mother came to help for the first few weeks. Then her husband stayed home from work for a few weeks after that on paternity leave. When he went back to work, Bridget's world spun out of control.

There was all the laundry to do, two babies to feed and change, the garbage, grocery shopping and sleepless nights. Bridget felt like she barely had time to comb her hair and get dressed. Time marched on and before she knew it, the twins were four years old. Toys had taken over the house. Bridget's beautifully organized home had devolved into a home overflowing with toys, laundry, and clutter.

On the morning that she took the twins to their first day of pre-kindergarten, Bridget came home, looked around, and cried. She wanted her home back. She was overwhelmed by the amount of disorganization and didn't know where to start. A friend referred her to Diane. When they spoke, Bridget told Diane the living room and kitchen were the two places in her home that bothered her the most. If she could get the children's toys out of the living room so that she could have a place to feel like an adult, that would be awesome.

As they worked together, it was apparent that Bridget knew how to be organized. Diane and Bridget worked together while the children were at school. They first reclaimed the kitchen. Then they organized the toys. Some toys were put up in the children's room. Some toys were put in a play area adjacent to the kitchen. Toys the children had outgrown were donated to a local daycare center. Any toys that were missing pieces or were broken were tossed. The clutter quickly disappeared, and Bridget reclaimed control of her home environment.

In their final organizing session, Diane worked with Bridget to create a housekeeping schedule. Together they put together a real-istic, simple plan for tackling household chores on a weekly basis. By rotating the chores, most tasks were scheduled at least once a week. Bridget felt like her old self once again.

Passive Decline

Passive decline in the aging population, while also not a medical disorder, can result in an environment that is over cluttered and perhaps even showing squalor. As a person ages, they may encoun-ter mobility limitations and diminished vision. They may find it more and more difficult to pick up dropped items, put possessions and purchases away. They may completely miss or have no real awareness of how their home is becoming hoarded. They may be less social as it is difficult for them to get out and go places, and they may be too embarrassed to have people visit them in their home. Many of these seniors may qualify for help in the home once a friend or family member realizes that help is necessary to keep the person safe in their home.

Olive's Story

Olive was a very intelligent woman, but one who depended on her husband to take care of household matters. Early on she had been a social worker and then moved into the field of special education as an aide. During that period in her life, her husband died. It was very hard for Olive to take over household management with all the paperwork and bill paying. She was very fearful of throwing away anything that she might need later. She was also very sentimental and liked to keep items that related to her family and her students.

Still, while her home was overcrowded, the kept items did not severely impact her lifestyle. She worked, went to church, and socialized. Then she started having physical problems. It became hard for her to bend over and pick things up and even to walk very far. Instead of putting things away or picking up some items when they dropped, she left items where they landed. Olive tended to stack items on the furniture and counters where they were easier for her to reach.

She had hip surgery which helped a little but still had difficulty with her mobility.

One night, there was a fire in her house. For people with large amounts of clutter, fires are a big concern. The fear of fire spreading is scary for everyone, but the fear of losing precious items is concerning for the collector as well. Fortunately, Olive's son was spending the night and he helped her get out of the house. After calling 911, the fire was put out but there was quite a bit of damage. Jonda reached out to see if her friend, Olive, wanted help and was invited to come in and help her put her house in order. This was an opportunity and an opening for both Olive and Jonda. Before the fire, Jonda had volunteered to help but Olive was too proud to accept. The fear and shame were too great, and she would minimize her need for help or the real concerns that her home wasn't as safe as it could be. After the fire and the amount of damage, it was easier for Olive to let go of items she really would have liked to keep but that she could finally see had no place in her life in the condition they were in.

But the opening was short lived. Not long after, Olive's health also declined. She had knee replacements and had a bone break in her leg near her hip. She spent time in a rehab facility; but when she returned home, she wasn't as mobile as she had been. She also lost her motivation to keep forging ahead in either her home or her physical therapy. Today, she is in a wheelchair most of the time and is beginning to show signs of dementia. Olive is housebound unless her son takes her somewhere, and her home is now so overstuffed that there are rooms in the house where a person cannot even enter. Some areas have only pathways to move through, but the livable space is completely taken up. Things are dropped and there they stay. Her son helps her as he is able; but the collective shame is too much and he refuses the help Jonda would like to give. As both a friend and a professional, Jonda would love to do more, but her weekly visits with food is all they are open to. Her worry is that if she pushed, the family would not allow her to do what she's doing now. The hardest part is that due to Olive's age and her insurance coverage, there is help available if the family would only ask for it. Jonda continues to hope that someday this will happen.

Collections Go Wild

Many people have or have had collections of items that have meaning for them. Children often collect rocks or feathers. If you are a traveler, you may collect spoons, teacups, or figurines from the places you visit. You may have a hobby or passion and √ have collected books on your topic. Not only do you add to your collections, but now friends and relatives "gift" you additions to your collections. If you keep adding to these collections over the years, they may begin to take over parts of your home. If every piece is "special" and nothing is ever discarded, the collection can go wild. The items no longer fit in cabinets or on bookshelves. Items may accumulate in boxes or stacks on the floor. Whole rooms may become dedicated to the collection and the rooms can no longer be used for their original purpose. This hoarding-like behavior will continue to manifest itself until the person realizes that the "collection" is disrupting their life.

If every piece is "special" and nothing is ever discarded, the collection can go wild.

Virginia's Story

Virginia's husband contacted Diane because they had a collection that had taken over part of their bedroom, the upstairs hall, his dressing room and Virginia's closet. He had had enough. He was ready to get boxes of trash bags and dump everything into the trash. He was overwhelmed by the amount of travel memorabilia and wanted it gone. This is not unusual. We often get calls from family members seeking help for their loved one. We always tell them the person to whom the things belong must contact us. We won't come in and remove belongings without the person working right beside us to make decisions about what stays and what goes. When Virginia finally called Diane, they scheduled an organizing session.

Virginia's collection was travel memorabilia. She saved every ticket, brochure, map, and trinket from every trip she and her husband had taken. As a couple, they traveled often, sometimes three to four times a year. Some trips were new, but others were revisits and so the saved items were often duplicated. Virginia understood her husband's concern and admitted she was overwhelmed by it all as well. She was also concerned about the possible fire hazard they had in the upper part of their house. The hallways were narrow and made even more so by the piles of memorabilia. Virginia had tried organizing some of the items into piles in her bedroom and his dressing room, but she completely gave up when it came to the items in her closet. There, she didn't bother at all.

Getting creative, Diane asked if Virginia had any interest in creating memory books or scrapbooks with the ticket stubs, maps, and postcards she had collected. Virginia thought this was a great idea. The first step was sorting the information and deciding what to keep. They gathered items from the upstairs hall and sorted it by travel destination. Virginia was willing to get rid of all duplicated maps, postcards and ticket stubs which was a great help and a quick fix. Diane brought large manila envelopes in which to put the sorted information. She labeled the outside of the envelope with the travel destination. Diane stored the manila envelopes in a cardboard banker's box. Bit by bit, the piles were reduced. The floor of the bedroom was reclaimed, and Virginia's husband's dressing room was completely clutter-free. Virginia decided she liked the idea of creating the scrapbooks so much that she was willing to remove the memorabilia from her closet also. Now, all of their travel memories would be kept in the same fashion. When Diane and Virginia finished working together, she was in the process of putting the scrapbooks together one destination at a time. Virginia and her husband cleared a bookshelf in their family room on which to keep these fabulous memory-filled scrapbooks so they could enjoy them for many years to come without the unnecessary piles cluttering their lives.

Medical and Psychological Challenges

Medical and psychological challenges can also be associated with hoarding. Severe ADHD (attention-deficit/hyperactivity disorder), OCD (obsessive compulsive disorder), Bi-Polar Disorder, PTSD (Post Traumatic Stress Disorder), Borderline Personality Disorder and Anxiety are some disorders that are frequently mentioned in conjunction with hoarding and hoarding-like behaviors.

Harriet's Story (ADHD)

Harriet is a professional woman. She has an office in town and a separate office in her home. She called Diane and explained that she has ADHD and an overabundance of paper. Each time she gets an idea, she knows she will forget unless she writes it down. So, she writes it down on a scrap of paper and walks away.

Harriet has endless important notes on scraps of paper all over her home. When it comes to her daily routine, she also has a hard time getting organized. Remembering what she needs to take with her in the morning is always stressful. Her wallet and her keys are often missing as is her iPad. Because of this, she's often late and feels chronically behind. Her goal working with Diane was to figure out a way to keep track of her notes, her wallet, her keys, and learn how to get places on time.

Diane and Harriet talked about what Harriet does when she first walks in her home. Together they found a spot for Harriet to always hang her keys near the door. Diane asked Harriet if it was alright to put a checklist on the inside of the door – the part you face as you open the door to leave. Harriet agreed. Diane made a checklist with Harriet of the regular things that Harriet sometimes left at home: her wallet, her keys, any paperwork for her office.

Next Diane suggested Harriet keep a small spiral-bound notebook with her at all times. Harriet could jot down her notes and they would be with her. She could also keep her notes in the notes app on her phone. Harriet liked the idea of the notebook better as she was a very visual person. If something was out of sight, she was bound to forget it. The trick with using the notebook was to refer to it. Harriet had to develop the habit of checking the notebook for the ideas and reminders she had written down. She also had to remove any out-of-date or completed notes. This took a little practice.

To help Harriet get to where she needed to be on time, Diane taught Harriet to do backwards planning. Instead of writing down when an appointment starts, Diane taught Harriet to write down the time she needed to leave to get to the appointment. Diane also asked Harriet to give herself an extra few minutes in case she was distracted by something along the way. The next step was to set an alarm in Harriet's phone a few minutes ahead of the actual departure time so that she would start to get ready to leave.

By the time Harriet's series of organizing sessions with Diane were finished, she felt more in control of her home and her daily life. She knew where to find her keys and her wallet. She had her checklist on the inside of the front door as a reminder before she left for work. There were no more random notes scattered throughout her home, and Harriet was mostly on time instead of being mostly late for appointments.

Andrea's Story (PTSD)

Andrea was working with a therapist who was treating her for PTSD. Andrea was concerned because there was clutter waist-high throughout much of her apartment. According to Andrea, both of her parents were hoarders. Andrea is someone who looks for support. She attended an event where Jonda offered a presentation on paper management and decided that reaching out would help her gain some control over the clutter in her life.

As they got acquainted, Jonda learned that Andrea worked seven days a week and lived alone except for her cat. She had recently come out of an unhealthy relationship with a man who she felt was a hoarder. Her goal was to reclaim her apartment and get control of her paperwork. Jonda worked with Andrea to help her clarify her goals. As they worked together, some patterns started to emerge. Andrea was very uncomfortable with open spaces. They worked on clearing a table next to the entry door that was stacked with items at least a foot high. As they got to work, things progressed well. They were able to sort some items together, throw some things away, and put some accessories elsewhere until the wood surface of the table began to show. But at that point, Andrea began to get agitated and wanted to stop work. As Jonda and Andrea talked through her feelings, they discovered that if items were spread across the table but maybe only stacked a little bit, Andrea felt better. She was willing to give that arrangement a try for a week.

The same thing happened when they were clearing a bigger area of her living room floor. Andrea shared that she was uncomfortable with the open space. Jonda put some empty boxes on the floor that had been cleared with the understanding that as she was able, Andrea would begin removing the boxes one at a time or replace them with something that was logical in her living room. They cleared off half the couch so that there was room for both Andrea and her cat to sit and rest. The other half of the couch held boxes of paperwork files. That arrangement felt better to Andrea, and she was willing to try and maintain that level of an "open space" to see if it could work.

Andrea and Jonda went through the same process clearing off the kitchen counter. Many items were left on the counter, but they were logical items and placed where they would be used. Most food items were moved off the counters to the cupboards to keep working on this theme of making "open spaces" tolerable.

By the time they finished working together, Andrea was satisfied with her living room and her kitchen. She felt comfortable having friends over and was happy with the way her space, paperwork, and life was now organized. Her goals were met.

In Conclusion

When you walk into someone's home and discover that it is filled up and overflowing, try not to jump to the conclusion that this is hoarding. Take time to listen, keep an open mind, and ask open-ended questions. Things are not always as they seem. It's not uncommon for emotional challenges to cause or impact a person's ability to keep their space organized or clean. A self-proclaimed diagnosis as a hoarder is not always appropriate. When in doubt, consult a therapist. But if the issue is chronic messiness or clutter that is motivated by other life circumstances, it is possible with guidance and gentle assistance to unpack the environment and return it to a safer and more organized way of existing.

CHAPTER 4

What Triggers Hoarding-Like Behaviors

Is this you? Your house has never been the type that would show up in a home decorator magazine, but you always felt that it was comfortable and just looked lived in. Then one day you looked around and asked yourself, "what happened?" The place looked like a bomb went off. There were clothes, both clean and dirty, in piles everywhere and draped over chairs. There were dirty dishes piled in the kitchen sink, on the kitchen counters, and scattered here and there around the living room as well as an empty pizza box and drink containers. The venetian blinds had so much dust on them that they looked flocked. The floor had practically disappeared under piles of newspapers, magazines, books, and other stuff with only paths to walk through the rooms. You know this did not happen overnight. How did your home get to the place where you were ashamed of the clutter and overwhelmed by the mess?

Well, in this, you are not alone. This has happened to countless numbers of people for a wide variety of reasons. These reasons may include illness, anxiety, procrastination, trauma, or a life-changing event.

Here are some short stories from our experiences with clients and how hoarding-like behaviors showed up. One or more of the situations may resonate with you and those you know. These fabulous people's homes came to be filled up and overflowing for many different reasons. You may see yourself in them, leading you to ask: could that be me?

Could that be me?

Roberta's Story (Medical Condition)

When Roberta called Diane, she told her that she had been thinking about calling her for almost five years. In the years leading up to the call, Roberta had been receiving Diane's newsletter and following her tips on her DNQ Solutions Facebook page. It took a tremendous amount of courage for Roberta to finally pick up the phone and talk with Diane. She was embarrassed and filled with guilt and shame about the condition of her home that she procrastinated calling.

During this phone conversation, Diane learned that Roberta had a medical condition which severely impacted her mobility and, of course, her ability to keep her house tidy. Combine this medical condition with a busy family and a tendency to be messy and you have a perfect storm.

Roberta has three grown children, two of whom still live at home. They are one of the reasons Roberta finally got up the courage to call. The children urged Roberta to reach out to Diane. They knew their mom needed guidance to get their home organized and were willing to help by providing the manpower.

When Diane arrived, it was apparent that there were no organizational systems in place. None of the belongings had a dedicated home. Kitchen utensils were mixed in with books, CDs and videos. Medicines and piano music were mixed in with office supplies. Files, bank statements, and medical folders were piled on the couch and on the floor near Roberta's favorite recliner in the living room. Clothes and shoes were scattered here and there. And then there were the cat toys and food. Mixed in with these things were empty mail order boxes which added to the disorganization.

Roberta's medical condition severely reduced her ability to move around the house. She is on oxygen, walks with a cane, and has a hard time reaching up high to put things away. Bending over to pick things up is also difficult. Any organizational system has to be simple so that Roberta can explain it to her husband who is very willing to help put things away. He just needs to know what to do and how to do it.

Diane's first job was to talk with Roberta. Actually, Roberta talked, and Diane listened. She heard about Roberta's vision for her home. She read many books on organizing and decorating and loved watching HGTV. Roberta had lots of ideas as to how she wanted her home to look at the end of the project. Her overarching goal was to create a peaceful and comfortable home for her family. Roberta explained she wanted to figure out how to assign homes to her belongings and then to learn how to maintain the organizational system. She never wanted this disorganized mess to happen again.

She knew much of what was laying around she didn't want. She just didn't know what to do with it. Almost more importantly, Roberta couldn't physically deal with it. With the children's help, Diane went around identifying all the things Roberta knew she didn't want and then put them into the empty delivery boxes and into Diane's car.

Over the next few months, Diane and Roberta worked together with Roberta's children to create order in the ground floor rooms, the entry, the living room, dining room, kitchen and master bedroom.

They cleared one area at a time, all the while talking about the way in which the space will be used from now on. Diane and Roberta decided what furniture and other items had to stay in the space to support the function of each room. The remaining items were removed.

The dining room was turned into a home office. Roberta was no longer going to host big family dinners, so she was eager to repurpose the dining table as a workspace. Once that decision had been made, it was easy to move things around and outfit the dining room with the remaining office supplies and file boxes. This allowed the living room to be a comfortable and relaxing space instead of a workplace.

Although Roberta's medical condition triggered much of the disorganization within the home, organizational solutions were put in place which helped Roberta realize her vision of a peaceful and comfortable family home.

This story has a happy and successful conclusion. Diane continues to work with Roberta occasionally to tweak the kitchen, the master bedroom closet, and the new office organizational plan. Not all stories have happy endings, as you will read in the next story about Doug.

Doug's Story (Trauma)

Doug reached out to Jonda because he wanted to organize and declutter the downstairs of his home, organize his paperwork, and add structure to his life. He told Jonda, "I just want my home to be in such good shape that my ex-wife will be comfortable letting my son visit."

While divorced, Doug was still in contact with his wife. He kept pictures and notes from his son on his refrigerator. When Jonda arrived for the first visit, it became apparent that the declutter process was not going to be an easy job.

His kitchen was unusable. Fast food boxes were everywhere. Counters were overflowing with dirty dishes, trash, old food, and papers. The dishwasher was full of dirty dishes that had been there forever. In fact, the dishes had to be removed from the dishwasher and soaked so they could be properly cleaned. The stove was not safe to use without a thorough cleaning. It was a fire hazard due to the buildup of splattered grease and crusted food droppings. Some of the food in the refrigerator was not edible. There were containers with mold and others that were past their expiry date.

Doug and Jonda sat down and made an outline of his priorities. Doug wanted his paperwork organized by topics. He had legal files, financial files, home information, medical files, and vital records scattered throughout the downstairs area. Papers and other materials covered the floor.

Jonda knew that this project was too big for her to do alone, and she got permission to bring in another organizer to help. As they worked, Doug shared information about his situation.

At one point he had been happily married and he doted on his son. He had been in the military and was now out on disability. He suffered from Post-Traumatic Stress Disorder (PTSD), Attention Deficit Hyperactivity Disorder (ADHD), and he has Traumatic Brain Injury (TBI) because of an accident three years ago.

Jonda and another organizer, Trish, worked with Doug several hours a week over many months with a few breaks in continuity. A lot of progress was made. Doug worked well with the organizers but needed constant redirection. Jonda and Trish got the kitchen in good order and Doug was sort of maintaining it with weekly assistance. The current papers were organized, and Doug could find them, but more papers kept coming in. The paper problem was compounded because Doug was not comfortable unless he had multiple copies stored in multiple files.

We believe his hoarding-like behaviors came from his lack of focus and his fear of losing his home. He constantly patrolled his area inside and out. He could not focus well enough to accomplish performing day-to-day chores in his home such as picking up magazines/reading material or cleaning the kitchen and bathroom areas. He could not drive so he paid others to take him to stores and the VA hospital.

Jonda wrote a letter to the VA hospital explaining Doug's circumstances, what she was observing, and suggested that Doug receive more financial assistance from the VA. The lawyer Doug was working with to secure his home seemed less and less available which was upsetting. Jonda connected Doug to the local Veterans Association, hoping he would find some local people who would assist, befriend, and understand him.

Work stopped when Doug contacted Jonda to tell her that he lost his home and was working to coordinate a move into a one-room apartment near his family.

In this case, it seems like there could have been a better ending if more assistance and advice had been available to Doug much earlier. And, of course, if Doug had been willing to accept the help and advice.

While Doug's situation is unusual, we find that many of our clients are challenged by procrastination and anxiety.

Margot's Story (Procrastination and Anxiety)

Margot and Diane know each other socially through volunteer community groups in which they participate. As is often the case when someone finds out that Diane is a professional organizer, they invariably say 'I need you to come live with me and help me with all my stuff.' Margot said something like that when they met. Diane thought nothing of it and never expected to hear from her professionally.

Diane was pleasantly surprised when Margot called and invited her to come and give an assessment. Margot and her husband live in a two-story home not far from Diane. The downstairs except for the kitchen was pristine. Nothing was out of place. The kitchen was a different story. There were stacks of cookbooks, magazines and newspapers scattered throughout. Every available surface was covered with pots, pans, baking equipment and other cooking accessories. Diane expected this because she knew that Margot likes to test recipes.

The tour continued upstairs. Margot's bedroom looked as if a tornado had swept in and disrupted everything on Margot's side of the room without touching the bed. There were papers, magazines, file folders, baskets, and a pen holder stuffed with pens and pencils all mixed in together. Very little was out of place on her husband's side of the room.

The two other rooms upstairs were also full. The guest room contained file boxes piled one on top of the other. There were also bags and bags and bags of receipts, a guest bed with more books, magazines and files piled on it, and a desk with more papers and files scattered about.

The next room was so full, it was overflowing. Things were stacked one on top of the other from the floor to the ceiling.

There were shopping bags with things to return to the store, broken kitchen appliances, clothes, and other unwanted things. Margot's husband's drafting desk and chair were visible in the corner. There was a narrow path between the door and the desk.

When Diane asked Margot about these rooms, she started to cry. She was embarrassed to show this side of herself to anyone other than her husband. He was frustrated because his office was so full that it wasn't a pleasant place to work. Margot knew she had to do something about all this stuff. She wanted to, but she was anxious about all the piles of paper and random bags of stuff. What to do with it, how to start, how long would it take, and how much would it cost were questions swirling around in her mind. She didn't want her home to look this way. Margot told Diane that she put off dealing with any of these rooms because she couldn't decide what to do, so she did nothing. What Margot didn't realize was that doing nothing is a decision in itself.

Thinking about what to do made Margot anxious. To rid herself of the anxiety, she put anything she didn't know what to do with in a bag and in another room so she could shut the door on it. It was almost as if she made these things and these decisions go away, which is what she really wanted.

It was clear that there had been a shift in Margot's thinking, or she would not have invited Diane over. She was looking for a solution. Diane let Margot know that her home had not become this way overnight. It was not going to be fixed overnight either. Together, Diane and Margot made a prioritized plan for tackling the different areas upstairs. They made a plan and set up a regular schedule to work on the piles. Diane gave Margot suggestions of what she could do in between organizing sessions to move this project along which would reduce the cost. Margot realized that making decisions, reducing the piles, and opening up the spaces was not as difficult as she anticipated. The more she worked on this project, the more in control she felt which in turn reduced her anxiety.

Margot's anxiety was linked to procrastination and to delayed decisions. Sophia's anxiety is completely different and is more complicated.

Sophia's Story (Depression and Anxiety)

Sophia called Jonda because she wanted to organize her two-bedroom apartment hoping to move. When Jonda arrived, she could easily see why Sophia needed help. There were only paths throughout the apartment because of stacks of books, magazines, and papers. Sophia likes to look through magazines and clip pictures and articles on a variety of topics. She has a very difficult time letting go of printed material. She feels like the printed word is her lifeline.

Sophia shared that although she has Post Traumatic Stress Disorder (PTSD) as well as a Traumatic Brain Injury (TBI), she also has a lot of strengths. She has a high verbal IQ, can communicate easily, and is very friendly. When she was young, she used to have a lot of friends. Her difficulty, according to Sophia, is with spatial learning which means that she has difficulty perceiving, analyzing, and understanding visual information in her environment.

Sophia told Jonda that she was born into trauma. Her mother's father died nine months before she was born, and her mother was grieving. Sophia was the oldest of a large family and was responsible for much of the work done in the home. Sophia was often sick as a child. She remembers being told that she almost drowned when she was three. Sophia has a lot of anxiety from trauma that was not resolved. She feels that all these events and more have contributed to her current condition.

Growing up, Sophia did not collect things, but she may have had more books than her friends. She liked to spend long hours in the library researching and trying to find out the whys. At one point, because she spaced out a lot, she was diagnosed with Temporal Lobe Epilepsy (a chronic disorder of the nervous system characterized by recurrent, unprovoked focal seizures that last about one or two minutes). However, she never had a seizure.

Later, that diagnosis was changed to Parietal lobe dysfunction. The parietal lobe plays a key role in integrating sensory information like the knowledge of numbers and their relations. Sophia felt that this was why although she easily could get a job, she had a tough time holding one. She worked several years at a bank but was finally let go. In the 60s, she developed a cognitive disability or loss of function that hindered her ability to perform mobility tasks which resulted in her losing her license and not being able to drive. For most of her life after that, she felt like she was in a prison because she couldn't drive and had to depend on others to take her anywhere.

Since Sophia feels trapped in her home, she believes it is hard for her to get information which is her way to protect herself.

She does not own a computer and, for that matter, does not even know how to use one, although her dream is to learn. Books and information are like a drug to her. In her words, "It 'Band-Aid's' me," and "My disability is a hidden disability." Sophia goes on to say, "I can go out on the street and no one would suspect or understand what was going on with me." She rarely leaves the house because of her fears.

Sophia is aware that she must let go of much of her collection of books, papers, and research in order to keep her apartment up to code and to make it easier at some point in the future to move. She is trying very hard to do the right thing.

As of this moment in time, Sophia is continually trying to let go but it is painful for her because of her fears and anxiety. She is talking about learning some basic computer skills so that she can look up current information instead of bringing in more hard copies. When she does move, her dream is to live near a library.

The preceding stories have talked about hoarding behaviors triggered by anxiety. This story is completely different as it talks about hoarding behaviors triggered by a physical disability.

Franny's Story (Poor Vision)

This is one of the jobs on which Diane and Jonda got to work together. Franny called Diane because she has a jewelry making business and wanted help getting her materials and papers organized. She admitted over the phone that she is legally blind and that she has always been messy. As the intake interview progressed, Diane realized that this was a job for more than one person. She asked Franny if it was alright to bring a couple of other organizers along with her to the appointment. Franny agreed provided the other organizers always let her know what they were doing.

Diane reached out to Jonda and one other organizer.

Diane walked through the home with Franny. Jonda and the other organizer waited outside. Diane wanted to get a sense of where to start and how to organize the team before she brought them in.

The home had a living room which was just moderately disorganized. The kitchen and dining area were full of things scattered on the floor (which were tripping hazards) and on every tabletop or counter. It was clear that Franny dumped anything that came into the house on the first available surface without any thought of where that item belonged.

There was a large brightly lit workroom, her bedroom plus a second bedroom and a bonus room. The second bedroom had tables set up with many small jewelry accessories and tools piled about and stacks of unopened boxes. The bonus room was filled with boxes and boxes of colorful beads which needed to be sorted according to size and color. Franny had all the necessary containers and shelves. She just didn't have anything sorted or put away. Franny also stored her decorations, display cases and other things to use when she went to craft shows in the bonus room.

As Diane looked around, she could see why Franny was in dire need of assistance. Her poor vision made setting up an organizational system imperative to the success of her blossoming jewelry business.

It appeared that there were no set places to put her things. Consequently, Franny didn't know where to begin looking for what she wanted. Another result of the disorganization was that Franny had many more supplies than she needed. She regularly ordered more beads and jewelry accessories because she didn't know what she already had in stock. This tendency contributed to the hoarding-like behavior that resulted in bins and bins of every colored bead imaginable.

Diane decided to divide the team up. Franny went with Diane as she assigned places for Jonda and the other organizer to begin working. This gave Franny a clear idea of what each person was doing.

The team worked for several months. We created organizational systems for every area of Franny's home. As the beads were sorted and categorized, the tools and bits and bobs containerized, and the papers sorted, Franny's home came together. There was a place for her to assemble the jewelry, a place to find the different tools, beads and accessories, and a place for her to store her supplies for craft fairs.

In a best-case scenario, Franny would have a maintenance plan in place with someone coming in at least monthly to keep the system working. However, as is often the case, money was tight, so Franny had to maintain the organizational systems on her own. Both Diane and Jonda follow Franny on Facebook and can see that her business is doing well because she continues to have items up for sale.

Franny's hoarding-like behaviors are a consequence of a physical disability. In the next story, Shirley's hoarding-like behaviors were the result of a life-changing event.

Shirley's Story (Life-Changing Event)

We first introduced you to Shirley in Chapter 1. She had been seeing a therapist because she needed someone to talk to when she moved to Atlanta. You see, she was recently divorced, moved from a large house in another state to a small two-bedroom apartment in Atlanta. Add to all of this, Shirley's mother had never taught her any home organizational skills. In fact, Shirley called her mother a hoarder. The home in which Shirley grew up was full of stuff and always very disorganized. When she married, her husband (who was ultra-tidy) kept their home organized but didn't take the time to teach Shirley these skills.

The only thing Shirley told Diane when she called was that she was afraid she was going to be just like her mother. Shirley went on to say she didn't want to live like that, surrounded by stuff, never knowing where anything is.

When Diane arrived at Shirley's apartment door, she could immediately see why Shirley was upset. There were open, half unpacked boxes lining the narrow apartment entry. More boxes and furniture were stacked up to the ceiling in the second bedroom, papers were piled high on the small dining table, the kitchen counters were littered with things, and Shirley's bedroom had clothes everywhere – on the bed, on the floor, and in the bathroom. Diane knew she and Shirley had their work cut out for them, or so she thought.

Shirley had not told Diane much of her history before she came to the first appointment. As they worked together, Diane learned about Shirley's recent divorce, her move to a new state, and her new job. These life-changing events have huge impacts. Just one of those life-changing events would be enough to cause a disruption in someone's life. All three combined are a nightmare.

Shirley hadn't given much thought to the things that went into her move to Atlanta. As she and Diane unpacked the boxes, they came across some items which were broken, and some that Shirley didn't want. Things that were broken were tossed, boxes were emptied, cut down and recycled, and things were put away. Anything that Shirley didn't want was put aside for Diane to take to a donation site.

It turns out that many of the clothes that were on the floor were the wrong size or Shirley just didn't like them anymore. They were quickly sorted into two piles: sell and donate.

Diane worked with Shirley to organize her home in a way that made good sense to Shirley. She also created a home maintenance routine for Shirley to follow.

Organizing Shirley's home did not take as long as either Shirley or Diane originally thought. Shirley was not, as she had suspected, turning into her mother. Her disorganization was the result of three life-changing events and not having any basic organizing skills on which to rely. Working with a professional organizer enabled Shirley to create a home in which she was organized and comfortable.

In Conclusion

Many people will experience a time in their lives when they exhibit hoarding-like behavior. These situations are often triggered by physical or mental disabilities, a disruptive event, or a lifestyle change that causes a person to feel trapped, paralyzed and suddenly the "stuff" in their personal space adds up. Quite often when this happens, the person is so overwhelmed by dealing with the change in their life that they don't have the wherewithal to also deal with the stuff. They wear blinders and the stuff just multiplies.

The stories we shared give insight into situations that trigger hoarding-like behaviors. Before condemning this behavior in someone, try to discover the root of the problem or the initial event. Shame, paralysis, and self-consciousness may have taken over the person's life and have caused them to give up. These people are not lazy or uncaring. Understanding the "whys" may help you to accept the person and develop strategies to help unpack the stuff.

CHAPTER 5

Treatment Challenges for Hoarding-Like Behaviors

We know that there are many factors that can upset the balance in someone's life and cause hoarding-like behaviors. Ask any professional and they will tell you that treating a person with any of these behaviors is rarely easy. The challenges are many and difficult but not impossible to overcome.

Unrealistic Perceptions of the Degree of Clutter

Most people, especially those with hoarding-like behaviors, have an unrealistic perception about the degree of clutter in their home and the negative impact it has on their lives. Often when Diane and Jonda go into a home filled to overflowing with clutter or even one that is just a little disorganized, they hear one of these responses:

The client says, "This is probably the worst you have ever seen," or "Please tell me this is not the worst you've ever seen." Conversely, they might say, "Well, this is not too bad. At least it's clean," or "It's not as bad as those people on the Hoarding Show."

✓ Many people with hoarding-like behaviors are unable to see that their home is so filled with clutter that it is now unhealthy or unsafe. Since they do not view their clutter as a problem, they don't know how to judge the degree of clutter without help. Sometimes just taking pictures of the hoarded-up areas and having the person look at them is eye-opening. This is really not so surprising. Close your eyes for a minute. Think about the room in which you're sitting or standing. Before you open your eyes, think about the things you expect to see in the room. Now, open your eyes. Probably you see things in the room you did not anticipate. Quite often we are so accustomed to our spaces that we don't see what's there unless we're intentionally looking. This is why taking a picture of a filled up space and then showing it to the person who lives there is so valuable.

Quite often we are so accustomed to our spaces that we don't see what's there unless we're intentionally looking.

Using clutter/hoarding scales (see References: Useful Tools for details) is another way of helping someone figure out whether or not they have a real problem. We use two of these scales. The first is the Clutter Image Rating scale created by Dr. Randy Frost. This scale consists of pictures of different rooms found in a home that is filled with varying amounts of stuff. A person points to the picture they think best illustrates the level of clutter in that room in their house. Their self-assessment gives a strong indication for how they "see themselves" and their challenges.

The other scale is produced by the Institute for Challenging Disorganization (ICD) and is the ICD Clutter-Hoarding Scale®. This scale rates your home using several metrics. We have put both of these scales in the Resources section. Take a look at them to get an idea of how they might help.

Talking with a trained professional can also help someone challenged by hoarding-like behaviors to reach an understanding of their level of clutter. Finding out how "big of an issue" the hoard is can be a relief to them and lift a great weight off their shoulders if they discover the problem is not as bad as they first thought.

Unrealistic Perception of Time to Remediate

But still, the clutter is there and must be handled. After seeing some of the hoarding TV shows, clients often think that we can wave a magic wand and instantly put this house back into reasonable order in just a few weeks. After all, when they watch the hoarding TV shows, order happens in the space of an episode or two. What they do not show on these episodes is the large team of people working behind the scenes to create this miracle in just a few rooms, not the whole house. How long the project will take in reality depends on a great many things.

1. The attention span or energy level of the person

2. How much the person can do independently

3. How much help they can get from family

4. How much money can be spent on getting outside help

5. If the person will accept outside help; if there is trust

6. Outside deadlines like possible eviction

Keep these things in mind as we share some short vignettes to illustrate a variety of challenges we have come across in our work.

Scarcity of Money

In the fall of 2019, right before Thanksgiving, Diane answered a call from an elderly woman who was looking for assistance in her hoarded home. Trudy told Diane that she wanted to have an assessment done as quickly as possible because there was no heat in her home. She said it would be so wonderful if she could get the furnace fixed before Christmas. Please could she schedule an appointment with Diane ASAP so that there was a chance of making that happen. Diane happily agreed and went to see Trudy the very next day.

When Diane got to Trudy's apartment, she realized there was little chance of getting the furnace fixed quickly. In the initial phone call the day before, Trudy told Diane that her home was full and that she had limited funds to pay for remediation. Before seeing the home, Diane had been hopeful that she and Trudy could put together a team of friends or parishioners to support getting Trudy's home in order. Specifically, Diane knew that to get the heat working, they needed to minimally move enough stuff to allow a repairman access to the furnace. Upon arrival, it was clear that there was scarcely enough room for Diane and Trudy to stand together inside the living room, let alone for anyone else to work on the project.

The kitchen was impassable. There were only a few very narrow paths through this small apartment to Trudy's bedroom and the second bedroom. Trudy told Diane she was in the process of donating lots of clothes and had for the first time in years organized her closet. She showed Diane her closet, and it was absolutely perfect. It was the one place in the apartment that was completely clear of clutter. The rest of her home, however, was completely filled up. Furniture that was too big for the space was crammed into each of the tiny rooms. It was piled almost to the ceiling with smaller pieces of furniture and accessories, like pillows, throws, and knick-knacks.

Diane told Trudy to continue working on the paths and she would be able to let someone in to replace the furnace. But there was no room to bring in a team of people. Trudy had totally underestimated the amount of stuff in her home, the time it would take to resolve the problem, and the cost. She realized this as she and Diane were looking at the different spaces in her apartment. The very act of bringing someone new into her home to assess the situation allowed Trudy to remove her blinders. She finally saw her surroundings for what they really were. Trudy said she was going to work through the winter and clear everything out that she didn't want. She planned to save a little money each month and then call Diane back to help her organize her home from top to bottom. Diane hasn't heard from her yet, but you never know. Sometimes people call years later.

Lack of Trust

When a person affected by hoarding-like behaviors allows someone else in their space, they are trusting that this person will keep their secret. They trust this person will not be horrified, or ridicule them, or shame them. And they trust that this person will not run out and tell everyone about the disaster lurking inside the home. But perhaps most importantly, they trust that this person will NOT throw anything out without asking.

Having faith that the person will not toss anything without permission is a HUGE deal. We cannot stress that enough. It's a very big deal for one person to let another inside their home when the person is filled with guilt, shame, and embarrassment. Here's a story in which there was a big violation of this sacred trust.

Stacy has a problem with hoarding. She is married and has a couple of children. Stacy and her friend, Cynthia used to have coffee most mornings at Cynthia's house after the children went off to school. Stacy told Cynthia she couldn't come into her home because it was such a mess. As time went on, they became good friends. Stacy shared more details about the problem she had organizing her home. She allowed herself to be vulnerable with Cynthia and then asked if she had time to help get her home organized. Cynthia happily agreed. Stacy's husband had been asking her to do something about the living/dining room. He wanted the family to be able to have family dinners sitting at the table and the living area was too full of stuff. There was no place to sit and relax. In fact, the whole downstairs was a disaster. So, Stacy thought if Cynthia could help her get that area organized, her husband would be happy, and it might motivate her to organize other areas of the home.

The two women decided to spend a couple of hours a day working together in this living/dining area to clear the table and get the room together. As a reward for her hard work, Stacy's husband decided to take the family away for the weekend. Cynthia asked if she could still come over and do some organizing while the family was away. She wanted to help her friend make even more progress. Stacy agreed because she trusted her friend.

In the process of organizing, Cynthia found a stack of old spiral-bound notebooks. They were in the corner, behind a chair and under a stack of very old magazines. They were covered with dust, sort of ratty-looking, and all the pages had been written in. Without further consideration, Cynthia tossed them in the trash along with the old magazines.

When the family came home, Stacy and her husband were happy with the progress that Cynthia made until Stacy looked in the corner behind the chair. Years ago, Stacy had stacked her old spiral-bound notebooks there thinking that one day when she had time, she wanted to look through those notebooks. They were filled with short stories Stacy had written. Her dream was to read them, polish them up, and maybe one day publish them. She asked Cynthia about the notebooks and was crushed to learn they had been tossed in the trash. She couldn't believe her friend had violated her trust so completely. Needless to say, Stacy never spoke to Cynthia again.

It's hard enough for someone who is ashamed of their space to open their door and let another person in. It's a complete violation of trust if you throw anything out without asking first. Because you can't possibly know if something is actually a prized possession, it's imperative to always ask first. Moments like the one in the story are gone forever. Once trust is lost, it's next to impossible to earn it back.

Not Accepting the Process

Whether a person hires an organizer, a clean-out crew, or rents a dumpster for their front lawn, there is a process involved in cleaning out a home that is filled up and overflowing with stuff. When you hire an organizer, one of the promises of the service is that you can be sure that the things you want to keep will be found and set aside. This process takes more time because you will go through everything and ensure that valuables that may look like trash are not thrown away in the process.

Hiring a clean-out crew will make the job move along faster, but there's always a risk that they will miss some things. Because their job is to "clean things out," they may not look as carefully for things you want to save. Keep that in mind before signing off on a cleaning crew.

Finally, the least expensive way to get the job done is to rent a dumpster and park it in your driveway. While this may seem super-productive to some, the unintended consequences of using this method are that just tossing things in the dumpster does not involve the person who did the collecting or hoarding. They will not have learned any organizational skills or strategies. Once the clean-out is completed, the person who collected such stuff will likely do it again. Remember that this kind of behavior has a back-story. You don't want to forget the "why" in the equation out of a mere sense of "getting it done."

A study (link is in the References) conducted by The Recovery Village shows that cleaning out a hoarded home indicates the person will fill up the home faster than it was filled up originally. Sometimes a person with hoarding-like behaviors hires an organizer to help with this process without completely understanding what is involved or accepting that part of the process is to let go of belongings that are no longer serving a purpose in the home.

As a team, we worked with Jane for about 6 months. You may recall the story from Chapter One. Jane wanted to replace her HVAC and needed to bring in a repairman. Unlike Trudy, in the previous story, Jane was able to pay Jonda and Diane to work together for three hours at a time, sometimes more than once a week. Jane's home was so full that there were no paths to walk through in the home. The first time Diane went to the home, she squeezed through the front door, climbed on to a pile of stuff, swung her leg over the banister, and held herself in place on the pile by touching the ceiling. This was no small job. It was going to take time. Diane asked if she could bring in a second organizer to make the job move along faster.

One smart way to make progress is by having some guidelines to follow. We started this process by creating rules for Jane to follow. We made a couple of posters that listed the rules, so they were top of mind and easy to see. One poster had a list of things that could be tossed without asking. The other list included the special items that Jane wanted to save.

Not surprisingly, even though they had made these rules to follow, Jane was often reluctant to part with anything. She was seeing a therapist to help her with the decision-making process and yet, when it came time to donate clothes, books, CDs or other items, there was always a reason to keep them. In our work with Jane, we often cleared paths by creating piles of things so we could move through the space. These piles were inevitably knocked over and new ones had to be constructed. Some progress was made by putting back issues of magazines in large industrial trash bags and storing them out of sight, but progress was slow.

At the end of the six months, we had a meeting with Jane. Our conclusion was that we were continually sorting and piling the same things over and over, but very little was actually leaving the home. We didn't want Jane to keep spending money on a project that was going nowhere. Part of the truth everyone had to face was that Jane was not accepting that part of the process involved in releasing some of her belongings. She was lacking the willingness to embrace the concept of keeping what you use/love and getting rid of the rest. The challenge was that while she knew she didn't want to live this way, Jane was unable to accept that to remediate her situation, the process involved releasing the excess of stuff. It appeared that she was more invested in the feelings created by bringing new stuff home versus the relief of making her home safer and easier to manage.

The Addiction of Hoarding-Like Behaviors

Hoarding is similar to an addiction. In many circles, the deeper connection between compulsive shopping and hoarding is gaining attention, and research to see what connections exist between the two are being explored. As professional organizers, we do not diagnose our clients in this way, but the similarities to addiction bear some discussion. Here's what we see. The person exhibiting hoarding-like behaviors feels a desperate need to surround themselves with things. It's compulsive and often when we ask clients why they purchase their items, they do not have concrete reasons. They say things like: "My grandchildren would love this!" "It was on sale; they were practically giving it away." "This was too good to pass up."

In their discussions with us, clients share that the act of searching for things to acquire makes them feel good and provides a kind of high that they both seek and take measured actions to make time for. They also spend valuable resources on stuff without consideration of the consequences. As many clients have shared, they don't see their space filling up, and even when they do, the compulsion to shop and acquire doesn't recede. The knowledge alone that their home is unsafe, overflowing, or causing their loved ones stress does not inspire them to take action to either stop or clear things out.

This quote below is from a client and gives great insight into what it feels like for the person in this situation. This is the pain some people feel when they attempt to stop hoarding. For many, hoarding-like behaviors are so hard to change because it's like self-medicating or retail therapy. It fills a void.

"Cleaning out doesn't fix the other issues. It doesn't provide friends to help with the loneliness or isolation. Nor does it fix the underlying problems in relationships. It doesn't help me feel less anxious about my job. The shopping and accumulating things distracted me. I miss not having to think about my problems because I was so focused on getting the best deals. I know the hoarding has to stop and that it is unhealthy, but I miss it."

For a person in this situation, working with a therapist while also working with a professional organizer, trusted friend, or family member can bring about a successful conclusion.

Backsliding

Backsliding is a common problem for many people who are trying to get organized. They try a method for a while, stop, and then disorganization reappears. A couple examples of backsliding are organizing systems designed but not in use and piles of things brought inside and dumped.

Jonda was called in to work with Vivian because she was leaving for a business trip and needed to hire a pet sitter to take care of her cats. She was worried that the sitter might fall because of all the clutter in the home. Vivian and Jonda worked a couple of sessions and they were satisfied that the sitter would be safe. Vivian loved the progress and wanted to continue to work to reclaim her home. She and Jonda worked for two-and-a-half hours every two weeks for about three months. Then in the next session, Vivian told Jonda that she had been sick, and the clutter had returned. There was major backsliding. Once again, the living room floor was covered with bags of mail and boxes of cat food. Dirty dishes were on the end table. Vivian's work bag was dumped in a corner.

This became a pattern. They met once or twice a month. Vivian would make progress, then she would either become ill, go on a business trip, have a family crisis, or some other challenge would arise, causing the clutter to return.

Major backsliding occurred each time she had a crisis. Again, mail was in boxes and bags on the floor, more cat food and items purchased but not put away, holiday decorations (depending on the time of year) either not yet in place or waiting to be put away.

In this case, a little bit of backsliding would occur prior to each organizing session. Usually it was a small amount of mail and a few purchases which were dealt with quickly. Vivian became discouraged by her lack of progress. Thankfully, Jonda had taken pictures at the beginning of the project as well as others along the way to show Vivian's progress. As Vivian got discouraged, Jonda shared these pictures to show that while some backsliding had occurred, overall significant progress had been made. Vivian could see that there was much more floor space. Some furniture had either been removed from the living room or from the house entirely. File boxes were now set up on carts and scooted under a table instead of in the middle of the room.

Jonda and Vivian began keeping a running dialogue on the "why's." Why was there so much clutter? Why was it that Vivian could not do this without Jonda by her side? These questions and more were often asked. Vivian always apologized for her failures and soon began to understand that she was trying to do too much. Vivian accepted that some household standards could be "good enough." She no longer felt she had to wash down each item before either donating it or taking it to storage. She took some time at the end of the day to relax and reward herself for what she had accomplished. By letting up on herself and by starting to "see" her progress, things started to work better.

Vivian started to finally see that she had more stuff in her home than could be stored on shelves. She started donating things which created more space and clearer thinking.

One item that was a constant challenge was her cats. Jonda helped Vivian see that one task that brought her down was the ongoing job of cleaning items that were stored on the floor. The problem was that Vivian's cats liked to pee on things that were left there, creating a cycle of "never-ending cleaning" and a sense that "things were never done." The solution was to create opportunities to move items off the floor and onto shelves or in closets so that the cats were more likely to use their litter boxes.

The biggest shift of all happened when Vivian began acknowledging the things that she was doing right. Per normal, each session with Jonda started with a recap of what was going well and overtime, this list began to grow. Vivian stopped ordering so much online; in fact, she has almost stopped impulse buying entirely. Items are leaving the house faster than they are coming in.

Currently, Vivian is still a work in progress, but the prognosis looks good. The main point is that the long-term solution Vivian was looking for was found by being both realistic and practical. It takes time to resolve situations like this. Doing so allowed both women to understand why there was backsliding, discover the deeper reasons why it occurred, and then begin to build new thought processes and habits, creating a happier home for Vivian.

The long-term solution Vivian was looking for was found by being both realistic and practical.

Failure to Recognize the Negative Consequences of Hoarding

If the person doing the hoarding doesn't recognize the negative impact that hoarding is having on their life, then treatment is rejected. They may think to themselves, "This is my home and I don't see anything wrong with it. I like it the way it is." They may not understand they are endangering themselves. When stuff collects into piles on surfaces and on floors, it's hard to keep the home clean.

Dust, mold, and pet dander accumulate and then there may be poor air circulation, particularly if vents are covered and the windows shut. They do not recognize that this combination of particles can get into their lungs creating a health hazard. When they go to a doctor because of their health issues, it is unlikely that they will disclose their living conditions. They might not even make the connection between the home environment and their asthma or respiratory problems. While they may get some help with their breathing, the hoarding issue will probably not be addressed.

People who hoard may also have poor eating habits if their kitchen counters and refrigerator are overflowing. They forget to look in the pantry or refrigerator to see what they have before shopping. Food piles up in the refrigerator and expires. It just sits there rotting. Piles may have accumulated on the kitchen counters, in the sink, on top of the stove, and even in the oven. So, they resort to take out. They may see the negative impact on their budget or weight gain but will tend to blame it on being too busy or exhausted from work. They are not likely to make the connection to their hoarding-like behaviors for this problem either.

The challenge in treating a person who fails to recognize the serious nature of these issues lies in getting them to acknowledge their hoarding-like behaviors and the ripple effects they have on their life.

These effects extend to the immediate family quickly. Often spouses are culprits, but if their spouse is not engaged in hoarding-like behaviors themselves, the spouse tends to grow frustrated with the lack of control over their living environment. After repeatedly trying to manage the clutter with little or no success, the spouse may leave the relationship or stand ready to go. When the person doing the hoarding recognizes that their marriage is in jeopardy, this may be the consequence they are willing to pay attention to. Only from that place is change possible.

If there are young children in the family, they grow up and become desensitized to clutter. They learn to conceal their way of living from their friends and often don't learn basic life skills like cleaning, organizing, or categorizing. The person with the hoarding-like behavior may not acknowledge what is going on in their children's lives because they tend to isolate themselves from others. This lack of insight and awareness causes the parent with this challenge to miss the signs around what their child(ren) are dealing with at school and in their social world. If the children are odiferous or have dirty clothes, teachers or the school nurse may ask why. Kids tend to lie in these uncomfortable situations and come up with excuses to explain the odor or messiness. They will do this if their peers make fun of them too. The social impact on kids with these kinds of secrets runs very, very deep.

As kids get older, they learn to hide what's going on at home from others because they fear they may be taken from their parents. If Child Protective Services is notified of the condition of the children's home, this is one consequence that can motivate a person into action. The prospect of losing their children is a strong motivator to work on reducing the hoard and improving the level of clutter within the home.

If not treated, that young person may grow up to repeat the challenges. But not everyone with this issue has a history of parents who did the same thing. In both cases, a young single person with this problem cannot invite friends or dates into their home. They make up excuses because they are ashamed and embarrassed to admit that their date or friends may not come inside because of the clutter and accumulation of stuff. Again, the motivation to find love or friendship may be the powerful motivator the person needs to work on clearing their home. If the desire to have friends or a relationship and not live a solitary life is strong enough, it can result in reaching out and seeking help. If they don't recognize the consequences of their behavior, they may become even more isolated and lonely and resort to bringing in more things to fill the void.

There are other social implications as well. Being chronically late or arriving to work or other important events unprepared or disorganized impacts a person's career and social standing at work. It's hard to get everything ready to get out of the house and to work on time when you can't find your keys, wallet, glasses, or other small personal items. Often, it's these small items that get easily lost in the piles of clutter. Hours of time is wasted looking for missing items, not to mention the multitude of distractions faced when seeking leads to other treasures found while searching. The opportunity here is that if a person begins to feel they might lose their job because of chronic tardiness or disorganization, this may be the impetus they need to ask for (and receive) help.

Finally, it's important to not lose sight of a person's inner mental state. Many people with hoarding-like behaviors report feeling depressed because they are overwhelmed, ashamed, and guilt-ridden because they don't know how to begin to clean it up. They feel they should be able to do this on their own, but don't know how to start or where to turn for help. Eventually, this may lead them to seek help from a counselor. With the right questions being asked and answered honestly, there is a good chance that they will eventually make the connection and look for additional treatment for their hoarding-like behaviors.

In Conclusion

The truth is that for people with hoarding-like behaviors, the challenges are many. The biggest issue for a person who wants to help is to recognize the hoarding may be a symptom of a deeper, more meaningful underlying problem. Listening to the person who finds themselves in this situation is a place to begin. Let them talk about the situation. It will be easier to help reduce the clutter if you have an understanding of what may have prompted the need to hoard. Then gently, patiently, and calmly see if you can help slowly declutter one small area at a time. In the next chapters, we'll show you how to do it, so you have the greatest chance of success.

CHAPTER 6

Reducing the Clutter

We have looked at some of the possible causes and triggers that make extreme clutter appear in homes. We know that clutter affects all of us in some way and at different times of our lives. Different people have varying levels of tolerance for clutter. The two of us have very different tolerance levels. Diane likes to have a few piles of papers on her desk to work on in her office. Jonda likes to have her desk completely clear of clutter. Each person will have their own definition of how much is too much. As we talk about clutter and methods to reduce clutter, think about how much clutter you and your family are comfortable having in your home.

Since we know the accumulation of clutter did not become overwhelming overnight, it will not be conquered overnight. Do not get discouraged. Reducing the clutter in your home is not a weekend project. It is not uncommon to feel that even after a lot of progress is made, that you're still left feeling frustrated that there's "more to do". Don't lose faith. This is normal. To help you, let's look at some strategies and guidelines to chip away at this overwhelming task. Just remember, these strategies can be applied to every area of your home.

Start with the End in Mind

Instead of focusing on what you do not like in your home, focus on how you would like it to look. Think about how you want to feel when you are in your home. Now think about the different rooms or areas within your home. Some areas may be used for a single purpose. Other areas may have multiple functions.

Take an honest look at the different rooms and areas in your home. You will feel differently about each room. How you want your bedroom to look and feel is different from how you want your kitchen area to look and feel.

Take on just as much or as little as you want.

Choose one room and stand or sit there for a while. Close your eyes. Really focus on how you want this to look and feel in a perfect world. Now, open your eyes. As you look around the room, decide where you want to start making some improvements. Do not try to conquer the whole room at once. Take on just as much or little as you want. It might be your bed and bedside table, or it might be the counter or floor in your kitchen.

Just put your focus on where you want to start and in your mind's eye see what you want to change to match your vision.

Have a Brainstorm Session

The next step is to write down everything that you want to change in this room. Remember, these steps can be applied to every room and area of your home. Write down everything you can think of, no matter how large or small. Do you need to remove trash in order to see what you want to keep? Do you want to move furniture around?

When brainstorming, the point is to generate ideas to solve the problem or make a change. You want to list a lot of solutions that you can edit later. Some ways to create ideas are:

Draw out your floor plan and define what happens in each area. If you are in your bedroom, decide where to put dirty clothes, where to exercise, where to place current reading material, where to put clean clothes.

Cut out pictures that represent your vision for the room.

Keep a running list of changes to make that you add to as new ideas occur.

Whether you write down groups of thoughts, sketch or cut out pictures, or draw a floor plan, it is a good idea to make a list of tasks. This list of tasks will be the basis for your plan of action.

Work Your Plan

"The secret of getting ahead is getting started. The secret of getting started is breaking your complex overwhelming tasks into small manageable tasks, and then starting on the first one."

~Mark Twain

You have your vision. Your bedroom is open and clear. All clothes and books are put away. There is nothing on the floor. The tops of your dressers only hold what you use and love. Your bed is freshly made up with clean sheets and inviting. You have a couple of good reads on the nightstand by your bed.

But, with eyes wide open, you look at the way the bedroom is at this moment. There are piles of clothes, both dirty and clean everywhere. Books, magazines, and mail are in stacks that are toppling over. An exercise machine sits in one corner of the room and it is covered with clothes. You can't even get to your closet. Your bed has just enough room for you to slide into at night while the rest of it holds more clothes, books, magazines, tissue boxes, empty and partially empty snack bags, empty cans, and dirty glassware.

This is overwhelming. You just want to shut the door and walk away as you have so many times before. That vision is impossible.

Break Down Large Tasks into Small Steps

 Start with just one thing. Plan to have the bed clear so that you can fully stretch out and enjoy it. Grab a trash bag and a dirty clothes basket. Have a box in which to put things that go somewhere other than in the bedroom. Gather up all trash and put it into the trash bag. Find all dirty clothes and put them in the clothes basket.

If you find stacks of clean clothes, take them near where they belong. If you have items that should hang in the closet, but you can't even get to the closet to open the door, stack those clothes in a box as near to the closet as you can.

Put all the mail and magazines in the box for leaving the bedroom. Add any books, unless you have a bookcase in your bedroom. Understand that as you remove these items, you are probably making a bigger mess in another part of your home. That is OK. You will eventually get to that area and can deal with the mess there another time.

When you are done, stand back and really admire that bed. Do not dwell on the rest of the room. Tonight, your reward will be a good night's sleep in your bed. Tomorrow, consider scheduling work on the bedside table.

Now that you have your start, go back to that brainstorm list of tasks to complete in the bedroom. Some tasks are:

- Declutter the floor

- Declutter the bed

- Declutter and organize the bedside table

- Declutter the tops of the dressers

- Declutter and organize drawers

- Declutter and organize the closet

Focus on just one of these tasks at a time. Break each task down into smaller steps. The whole floor may be just too much to take on at once. Divide the floor into sections and work on one at a time. Are the clothes on the floor mainly items to go into drawers, shelves, or hang in the closet? The answer to this question may lead you to your next task.

If much of what you find on the floor belongs in your dresser, then the next task is to clear out the dresser so there is room for these clothes. Do this task one drawer at a time. Designate one drawer for lingerie. Take out anything from that drawer that does not fit.

Ask yourself: is it full of holes, is it too stained to wear, and do I still like it? Remember to remove anything that goes into another drawer. Ask yourself these questions as you go through each of your dresser drawers and act accordingly. This will clear up space for what has not been put away. If you still can't get everything in, ask if you should release some items or if you need another set of drawers. The goal is to get all items off the floor.

Develop a Timeline

To keep this plan on track, develop a timeline. Put each of the tasks on an index card, a sticky note, or in a Word document. Order the tasks into what seems a logical sequence. You can always go back and change the order.

Pull out your calendar. What dates and times will you commit to working on these tasks? Schedule working appointments with yourself. Write these intended dates on your list and in your calendar. Honor these appointments. Allow some "wiggle room." Life does happen and something important may come up on a day you scheduled to work on a task. Just don't let everything that comes up take precedence over your appointment with yourself.

Gather All Supplies Before Starting

Before your appointed time, assemble everything you think you might need. A complete list of supplies to have on hand is in the Reference section. Having these supplies available will prevent you from losing momentum once you get started. Depending on the task for the day, some items might be:

- Trash bags

- Donation bags or boxes

- Boxes for items going elsewhere

- Boxes for paper designated to be filed, tossed or shredded

- Gloves/mask

- Hand sanitizer

- Vacuum cleaner and bags

- Cleaning supplies

- Something special to help you celebrate as you go

When working on a big project, it is easy to get discouraged by all that needs to be accomplished. It seems like no matter how hard you work, progress is slow. The amount of work left to do overwhelms us and we want to stop.

What is important to remember is that everything you have done so far is an accomplishment. So, celebrate it! Emptied one box of papers? Celebrate. Decluttered one drawer? Celebrate.

Then give yourself a rest and a chance to recharge and regroup. When you are ready, go to the next task.

For some, celebrating accomplishments is hard. We've been trained not to brag or be proud. We have been taught to downplay our accomplishments. After all, we're only doing what we should be doing. No big deal.

But the feeling of pride is easier to generate than willpower. If we are proud of what we have accomplished, then we are more likely to keep working on the project. Think back to some project you did for someone else. They loved what you did and not only praised you, they told others what a great job you did. The next time they asked you to do a project, you were more than happy to do it because you knew it would be appreciated. Do the same thing for yourself.

A large part of success is about your mindset. If you know you can have success, you will keep trying.

Focus on what you've accomplished, rather than the overwhelming list of what still needs to be done. Celebrate every success, no matter how small. Cultivate a "success mindset" to keep you motivated to KEEP GOING.

Another reason to celebrate success is that it feels good. Dopamine is released into our brain when we anticipate achieving and do achieve a goal. It feels good and we want more.

Then, when you've reached a stopping point, take the evening off. Read a chapter of that book. Buy yourself a flower. Visit with a friend.

Celebrate!

Maintenance Is Required

Once an area is organized and exactly the way we want it, it is tempting to sit back, relax, and think we never have to organize that space again. This idea can be true if, and only if, we maintain the organization we have put in place.

Remember the bed you cleaned off? Let's say you come into the bedroom with a basket full of clean clothes. In front of you is the nice empty bed. The perfect place to put that basket of clothes right now.

We get it. Here is a nice empty spot to put down the basket of clothes. It's also a good space to fold those clothes. But you want to maintain the work you did on the bed. If the bed is not already made, pull up the covers. Now take that basket, fold those clothes, and put them away. Return the basket to where it belongs. You have not only maintained the bed by keeping it clear; you have also accomplished another task by putting your clothes away. You should sleep well tonight.

Other Things to Maintain: Papers, Dishes, and Clutter

If you let papers pile up, dishes accumulate in the sink, and stuff collect in areas that you have decluttered, then you are back to square one.

One way to avoid this is to schedule routine maintenance. Another way is to think through the cycle of tasks.

Certain tasks have a beginning, middle and end. If you complete the cycle of the task, follow it through to the finish, you will maintain the organization you have put in place.

Think about dishes, pots and pans. The beginning of the task is meal preparation. You get out the necessary ingredients and any pots, pans or dishes. Then you make the meal and eat the meal. This is the middle of the task. The task is finished when everything is cleaned up and either put in the dishwasher or put away.

You can apply the same concept to laundry. Clean clothes come out of a drawer or closet and are worn. When you take them off, you either hang them up (if they do not need to be cleaned) or put them in the laundry basket. If you wash the clothes, they go into the washer, into the dryer (or are hung up to dry), and then folded and put away. The last step finishes the cycle.

Completing tasks keeps the organization intact. When you decide to delay finishing the cycle of the task, saying to yourself, "I'll do it later" and then forget about it, the system breaks down. There are several helpful mantras which can help keep you on track. They include: "don't put it down, put it away," "did I complete the task?" and "be a waiter" (waiters never have empty hands – they always bring something to or from a table). If you see something out of place as you pass through a room, carry it to where that item belongs. Posting reminders like these can help you keep the organization intact in each area you tackle.

In Conclusion

It is possible to make the vision you have for your home a reality. The trick is to stay focused on the organization of one room or area until that space is finished to your satisfaction. It does not happen overnight. If you want to organize the entire home, it can take days, weeks or months. There is no shame in asking for help if you are overwhelmed with all that is necessary to make your vision come true. Take the time to envision how you want your home to look and feel. Honor yourself and stick to that vision.

CHAPTER 7

Tips for Family, Loved Ones, Well-Meaning Friends and Community

We want to let you know right from the beginning that offering to help someone with hoarding-like behaviors is a wonderful thing to do. It is also difficult. This task of helping someone deal with all their stuff at their pace can try the patience of saints. You need to strap on resilience, fortitude, and your good nature. You may be working in the same room or even with the same pile of papers for weeks.

Prepare yourself to meet with resistance from the person you are helping. You may want to get rid of something that is broken; they may want to keep it because it can be fixed. You may want to open that closet and empty it; they may not be ready.

You know that you are strong and that you will do the physical heavy lifting, moving furniture or boxes, but also prepare yourself to be their rock when they need a shoulder on which to cry. Understand that your primary concern is for them to be safe in their home. It may never become as neat and tidy as you would like. Understand also that all decisions, and we do mean ALL, must be made by the person you are helping.

Now that we've warned you about the task ahead, we know that people with hoarding-like behaviors do not talk about their home situation with family or friends because they are filled with shame and embarrassment. It then takes some sort of event which forces the person to allow family members or friends into the home.

Understand that all decisions must be made by the person you are helping.

Some signs that may alert you that your friend or loved one has a problem with hoarding are:

- the person experiences distress when giving away items or even considering giving them away

- the person feels safer when surrounded by possessions or having a living space filled or blocked by stuff

Knowing these things may provide you with the opening you're looking for to ask for permission to help.

Of course, family members want to pitch in when parents or grandparents are having difficulty because their home is no longer safe since clutter has taken over. Siblings want to fly out and help their brother or sister who has just been released from the hospital but cannot go back to their home until it is made safe enough to rehabilitate in. Spouses want to clear out the house so their marriage can get on a more harmonious track and kids/family members are safe at home.

Family members may have had some suspicion that something was not quite right; but when they see the amount of clutter that has filled the home, they are shocked. They want to dive in and help, but where do they begin? Friends may notice a difference with an old friend because now they are either met at the door or in the driveway but not invited in. All get-togethers are at a restaurant or another public place. Blinds are always closed. Then an event happens, and the hoarding-like behavior is revealed.

Be Available, but Wait for the Invitation

Jonda had a personal experience with this, previously mentioned in Chapter 3. Her friend, Olive, had been in pain for years before she finally decided to have knee replacement surgery. Olive had worked in the same school system as Jonda. After Jonda retired, they kept in touch and visited each other often. Olive lived alone. But, because of her pain, it became increasingly difficult for her to clean her house.

She was also very sentimental and liked to keep things around her that reminded her of her work with children and of raising her own family. Olive had always been very sociable, but then she stopped having people over. She was too proud to ask for help in her house. It had been years since anyone but close family were invited in, so her friends had no idea how filled up with clutter her home had become.

One night, there was a fire in her house. The fire had nothing to do with the clutter. Apparently, a microwave caught fire at 2:30 in the morning. It was very lucky for her that her son was spending the night. He managed to get his mother out of the home and call 911. Olive would not have made it out without his help since there were only pathways from her bedroom to the door.

After the fire was put out, there was a lot of damage to the home. Items that had been stacked all over were now either scorched or soaked with water. This event forced Olive to come to terms with the fact that she had to have help. She knew Jonda had been trained to work with people who are challenged by overwhelming amounts of clutter. She invited her over.

Not everyone is as lucky as Olive to have a friend in the "know." Often, the signs are there, but without some clear understanding of how to help, a clean-up project like this one could become more traumatic than the fire. So where can you begin to help?

What to Do If the Invitation Doesn't Come?

Let's surmise that you think your friend or loved one has a problem with too much stuff. You think this because it's been a long time (years) since you were invited inside the home. This is very unusual. Your friend or loved one used to host parties or, at the very least, invite you in for a cup of coffee and a visit every now and then. Now, you get together at your house or at a restaurant. Something changed. You may not know what the trigger was, but you want to help. And, to do that you have to get inside the home.

If you ask, "Why don't you invite me in?" you'll inevitably get any number of excuses ending with "the house is a mess and I don't want you to see it that way." The best thing for you to say is "I am here for you. I know you don't want to let me in. I am here to make sure you are safe in your home. I promise not to judge or scold you. You probably do enough of that to yourself. May I come in?"

If the person says, "No," don't argue with them. That will probably make them dig their heels in even deeper. Ask them to think about your offer of help and that their personal safety is your primary concern. Let them know that you aren't going to give up and that you will revisit this question with them in the near future.

Eventually, You're in the House. Now What?

When your friend meets you at the door, smile and look at them directly. Keep your body in a relaxed open stance and let your arms hang down by your sides. This is important because your friend is most likely scared, nervous, and hesitant about letting you in. You want your body language to reflect that you are not a threat. Resist the urge to scan the entry, looking for a place to start.

Ask them how they are feeling right now. Listen to them. Watch their body language; it may speak louder than their words. While they might say "I'm fine," they may have their arms wrapped around themselves, holding themselves tight. This indicates they're nervous. Ask them where they want to start to reclaim their home. They probably have no idea. Everything may feel important, difficult and overwhelming. Help them figure out where to start by asking, "What's bothering you the most today?" They are likely to answer, "Everything!"

Before You Begin

Remember to focus on the person you are there to help and not the overwhelming amount of stuff. They are aware there is too much stuff in the house. Continually drawing their attention to it serves no purpose. Look at safety first. Ask if they have more than one exit which is easy to access. If they do, congratulate them. Tell them that you are really happy to know that entrances and exits to the home are clear of stuff and can be easily opened.

Another question about safety involves the air vents, heating ducts, and furnace. Making sure that the air can move about inside the home is important. It's also important to keep the area around the furnace clear. Ask if the two of you can take a little tour of the home. Look for the air vents and heating ducts. If there is something covering them, ask to move those things and explain why. Also ask if there is anything near the furnace. If there is, ask if you can move those things, too.

Please notice: we are asking you to ask the person. Always ask to see whatever. Ask permission before touching anything, opening any drawer, cupboard, or closet. Ask permission before moving anything – even a small piece of paper or a box that is in the way. Moving items from one place to another is distressing. Even though it looks like random stacks of stuff to you, they know where their possessions are and will become panicked if they cannot find them. They will think you tossed them, even if you just moved them.

Remember it has taken some convincing to get inside this home. You want to be able to come back so that you can help this person time and again make progress in their home. To make that happen, you need to earn their trust. You will have it if they understand you won't touch their things without permission.

As you walk through the home, subtly notice where the piles are the biggest. Where do you think is a good place to start? Ask if the person would like to start in that place. If they say no, ask where they would like to start.

Sample Scenarios and Conversations

Here are some possible scenarios and sample conversations. The ones you use will depend on each individual situation.

The Bedroom

The two of you are starting your work in the bedroom because the person wants to be able to sleep in their bed. The bed is covered in clothes. There are piles of clothes on the floor and draped over a chair in the room. The bedside table is piled high with books, magazines, tissues, and half-empty cans of soda.

Your focus needs to be on the bed since the stated goal is to sleep in the bed tonight. You say, "Let's take a look at the clothes on the bed. Do you like them?" The person answers, "Some of them don't fit and I don't know what to do with them." You say,

"Let's sort them. We can put away the things that fit and that you like. The things that don't fit or that you don't like we can put in a donation box. Is that alright? May I help by showing you each item? You can say 'keep' or 'donate' or 'I don't know.' O.K.?"

You take each piece of clothing and help by holding it up and waiting for the person to respond. It's O.K. if the answer doesn't come quickly. Allow some quiet time for the person to think. A great question to ask if the person is struggling to decide what to do with an item is: "Can you tell me more about this?" Maybe they aren't sure if it fits. If that is the case, make a pile of things to try on after you leave for the day. Then tomorrow, those clothes can either go back in the closet or be donated.

Resist the urge to share your opinions about the clothes. If you say you like the top or dress, the person will be more likely to keep it, even if it is something that doesn't fit that well anymore. This applies to everything in the house: paintings, photos, books – truly everything. Instead, complement the person on their efforts, acknowledging that this is difficult work.

If, after a couple of hours, half the bed is cleared, stop and celebrate. Suggest you both take a break. If the weather is nice, go outside for fresh air, green space, and a literal change of scenery. It helps to refresh and recharge you. Suggest that you each have a snack and some water before going back in to tackle the other half of the bed. The last thing that you want is for the person to make hasty decisions just to get it done because they are tired, thirsty, and hungry.

Let's suppose you go back into the bedroom after taking a break and you meet with resistance. The person doesn't want to clear anything more off the bed. They insist it's fine. They can sleep on half the bed.

You have two choices: you can argue (but, really you're not the one sleeping there, are you?) or you can ask, "Where would you like to work?"

The Kitchen

Here's another possible scenario. The person has decided they want to work in the kitchen. Every counter is cluttered with stuff. One kitchen counter is filled with open soda cans and a couple of drawers are partially open with stuff spilling out of them. You notice the stove top is piled high with magazines, flyers, and other assorted papers. The oven may have things (other than cooking implements) stored inside it too. You won't know unless you look. Please remember to ask before opening the oven.

There's a small table in one part of the kitchen piled with books and pantry supplies. Backpacks, tote bags, plastic grocery bags, and reusable grocery bags are hooked onto the backs of the two chairs. The floor has some piles of what may be trash mixed in with unopened boxes and canned foods.

The person tells you that they used to like to cook but now, of course, they don't even want to set foot in the kitchen because it is such a mess. Their goal is to be able to cook in their kitchen again.

Your primary purpose in helping is to make the environment safe for this person. Having said that, you don't want to begin with a judgment statement like: "You know, keeping magazines and papers on top of the stove is a fire hazard."

Acknowledge the person's goal and suggest the two of you start on the counter closest to the stove top. Tackle one small section at a time. Have a garbage bag handy, a recycling bin, and a box in which to put things to take somewhere else.

There's no need for lots of conversation. In fact, ask if the person likes music. Suggest playing the playlist on their phone. Do you remember the Disney musical *Snow White and the Seven Dwarfs*? The song "Whistle While You Work" comes from that movie. Playing music can relieve the intensity of this work.

Create some rules for these kitchen items. Suggest that any cans more than two months past their expiration date be tossed. Also, ask if you can put used paper goods or empty take-out containers in the trash.

The goal is to turn the kitchen back into a functioning room. To do that, you will first sort the things that are cluttering the counters, one counter at a time, putting things together and removing all trash. Then you will take the things that don't belong in the kitchen to the rooms in which they belong. The two of you will revisit those items another time. You will, with permission, empty the refrigerator of expired foods and look to see what, if anything, is inside the oven.

Reassure the person that whatever you see and whatever they say during your time together is confidential and remains between the two of you. It is imperative that you retain their trust for this work to move forward. They are taking a big risk exposing themselves and their home to you.

What to Say or Do When You Meet with Resistance

Let's say you're in the bedroom and you come across a handbag that is very well used. It looks like a critter has been nibbling at one of the handles and it has crumbs from a chocolate bar inside. You show the person the handbag. They say it is a keeper. You think it is obvious the handbag belongs in the trash. No one would want it. But the person you're helping wants to keep this handbag. What do you do next to get them to consider letting it go?

Ask the person to tell you more about the handbag. What is the story? There must be a story if they want to keep something that is in such a state of disrepair. Sometimes telling the story will help to release the item. You point out that it looks like a critter has been nibbling the handles and there are candy bar crumbs in the bottom. Ask if the person wants to take a picture to remember the handbag before letting it go. If that doesn't work, suggest putting the handbag aside while you work to declutter the bedside table. You will revisit the question before you leave for the day. Let them know, it is their decision. They may keep it but point out they will probably never use the handbag because it's damaged.

When you meet with resistance, there is no point in arguing. You can offer facts:

- Point out if something is broken, moldy, or damaged beyond repair.

- Point out they have x number of x and can only use one at a time.

- Ask how many they feel they need?

- Point out they only have room for so many things.

Ultimately, it is the person's decision to keep their things. Your only job is to make sure they are safe in their home.

If the person with whom you are working decides they are done for today, accept they have had enough. Making decisions about their belongings is emotionally and physically exhausting. They may be done before you think it's time to stop for the day. Accept their decision and make a plan for your next time to work together. They may need a couple of days or even a week to recharge before working again. It's important that you leave before you've outworn your welcome. Give them some suggestions of things they can work on, if they want to, before you meet again. If those things have been done when you come back, CELEBRATE! If they have not, say that's okay and move on.

Sometimes the person is not able to be in the house. They may be in a rehabilitation center or otherwise unavailable. In this case, it's even more important not to toss anything without their permission.

Misplaced Good Intentions

Here is an example of misplaced good intentions. A person may have been active in their church and have made lots of connections with the other parishioners. One day, they fall and break their hip.

They live alone and need to have rehabilitation in a nursing home. Their church family wants to help by cleaning up their home and stocking their refrigerator for their return. When the volunteers enter the home, they cannot believe what they find! They cannot see the floor. There are only pathways around the house and the refrigerator is overflowing with rotting food. They do not know where to start. They decide to put together a team to clear out the house of everything that is broken, clean the appliances, bring in fresh food, and maybe a bouquet of flowers.

You do not know what is precious to the person whose home you are cleaning up.

They feel good that they have helped make things right. While their intentions were good and honorable, what they did amounted to invading a person's home without permission. Their actions violated their friend's space by touching their personal property. When you put it that way, it does not sound like a good thing – does it?

Here is the thing: no matter how well intentioned someone is, going into another person's home to "fix it" according to the way you think it should be breaks the trust the other person has in you. It is a violation of the highest order.

You do not know what is precious to the person whose home you are cleaning up. For example, you might see dead flowers but for the person who lives there, they are the flowers from her mother's grave. This actually happened to a professional organizer we know. She was cleaning out a space with the person's permission. The two women were working in the den and the professional organizer picked up a bunch of dead flowers as if to put them in the trash bag. The woman stopped the organizer and said, "Please don't throw those flowers out! They are left over from when my mother passed away. I know I should toss them, and I will when I am ready. But I am not ready yet." Of course, she put the flowers back where she found them. Another example of this type of misplaced good intentions is included in Stacy's story.

Stacy's Story

You may recall this story from Chapter 5. Cynthia was helping her friend, Stacy, clean up and organize her home. They loved to chat over a cup of coffee. Stacy shared with Cynthia that she really needed some help organizing and cleaning up her home. It was full and she was ashamed to have anyone over; but because she trusted Cynthia, Stacy was ready to invite her in for some much-needed help and support.

Cynthia worked with Stacy over several months and they made good progress. Stacy was so comfortable having Cynthia in her home that when Stacy and her family were going out of town for the weekend, she invited Cynthia to continue doing a little cleaning up in the kitchen.

During the course of Cynthia's work, she came across a stack of ratty old spiral-bound notebooks. She casually flipped through a couple of the notebooks and noticed they were used. They had been written in. Cynthia saw no need to keep them. After all, they were ratty old used notebooks – clearly no one would want them. She put them in the trash.

When Stacy and her family came back from their weekend away, she noticed right away that the stack of notebooks was missing. The next day, Cynthia came over expecting Stacy to thank her for all the work she had done in the family's absence and was surprised by Stacy's question: "Where did you put the stack of notebooks?" Cynthia replied that she tossed them. They were old, ratty used notebooks, "Why do you want them?" Stacy replied that she had started writing short stories in those notebooks when she was in high school. This is something she had loved as a teenager. She wanted to reread some of those stories, rework them, and maybe publish them as a collection in a book. Stacy was crushed knowing that she could never get those notebooks back. She was also heartbroken because while she realized that Cynthia's intentions were good, she no longer trusted her. Stacy severed their relationship and never spoke to Cynthia again.

More Things to Consider

Be totally present when you are working with the person you are helping. Listen to what they tell you and be aware of their body language. They will be watching you for any sign that you may be judging them and the state of their home. Don't give them a reason to suspect you are. We do things without thinking some- times, like wrinkle our noses when we smell something we don't like. Control the urge to do that. If you have to, breathe through your mouth. Also, do not roll your eyes. These are small things that may send the wrong signal to the person. Keep your eyes focused on them when they are speaking to you. Put a smile on your face and in your voice.

Listen to their stories. These stories may offer clues as to what started this massive collection of stuff.

Maintain a positive attitude. Celebrate every time a bag is filled, whether it is trash or donations. You can have a special song that you play when this happens or just shout "Hurrah!" Whatever works in your situation. It's so important to keep the person's spirits up. You know the home will not be decluttered and reorganized overnight. There is no magic wand. It will take time, lots and lots of time and effort. It's time and effort well-spent. Because progress may be slow, it's important to celebrate each and every victory.

One way to relieve the person's feeling of being overwhelmed by all there is to do in the home is to make a spreadsheet, chart, or poster of all the things that the person wants (and needs) to take care of in the house. We suggest doing this as a brain dump at first. Let them talk and write down every action item. Then rank the items, beginning with the most important. You can make a beautiful poster or a more utilitarian chart or spreadsheet using your prioritized list. As the tasks are completed, cross them off. This provides a real visual motivator to keep the project moving. Understand that these are intentions and can be changed or modified as the project progresses.

Ensure that you don't become overwhelmed as you work to help the person reclaim their home. Don't work too many hours at a time.

Take frequent water breaks and refuel with snacks. Wear comfortable clothing.

If you are working as part of a team, assign one team member (team leader) to talk with the homeowner. The team leader can ask questions and then relay the answers to the rest of the team. You avoid confusion this way. The rest of the team must work silently as you don't want the homeowner to think you are talking about them. Our instinct is to chat and tell stories when we're working with friends. This chatter may result in laughter. You never want that laughter to be misunderstood by the homeowner.

Whether you're working alone or with a team, there are certain things you'll want to have available to you. You don't want to delay work in order to go shopping for supplies.

Supplies to Bring with You

Having some supplies with you will set you up for success. Bring an over-the-door hook and use it to hang your bag and personal belongings. It is easy to misplace your belongings in the clutter, and there is also the possibility of some contamination.

Keep the supplies in your car. Bring boxes or milk crates to use for sorting things or for carrying items from one room to the next. You also want to have a supply of garbage bags. Use clear ones so the person can easily see what is being thrown out or donated. Post-It Notes are good to have to label the outside of cupboards, drawers, and boxes among other things. Masking tape and a marker are important for distinguishing between garbage bags used for donation, trash and recycling. Only bring things in as you need them and ask permission before you do. A good reason to delay bringing things in until you need them is that they simply add to the visual clutter.

Also have a mask, hand sanitizer, and disposable gloves in your car, just in case you need them.

Continue to Educate Yourself

Look for online support groups on this topic. The benefit of participating in an online support group is that you are there with people who are experiencing similar problems. A good support group is a positive experience. People sometimes post before and after pictures in these online forums. You may get some good ideas of how to organize certain spaces with the person you're helping. You may also get some good ideas of what to do with things the person you're working with no longer wants to keep.

Read more books on the topic. We have a great list of additional books on the subject of hoarding and compulsive shopping in our Resources section.

If This Doesn't Work, It's Time to Look for Help

If you are making no progress in reducing the piles of things in your family member or friend's home, it may be time to seek professional help. Before you suggest a particular therapist, psychologist or counselor, read their background information to make sure they are taking clients who exhibit hoarding-like behavior. You may even want to call the office to find out how the sessions are conducted. Ask: "Does the person come to the home or are the sessions only in the office?"

Another type of help to enlist is a professional organizer. Not all organizers are educated about chronic disorganization and hoarding-like behaviors. If a professional organizer has experience in this area, it will most likely be evident on their website.

In Conclusion

Witnessing hoarding-like behaviors can be scary for family and friends. It can also be frightening for the person affected by hoarding. Oftentimes, when we don't know what to do, we either get stuck and do nothing, or we rush in seeking to just make things better - no matter what - do something! It has been said, knowledge is power. Reading up on the Hoarding Disorder will help. Learning to approach this disorder with compassion and a healthy dose of common sense will not only help to keep the relationship alive, it will also help reduce the hoard.

CHAPTER 8

Tips for Social Workers, Professional Organizers & Other Professionals

Social workers, psychologists, psychiatrists, and professional organizers have very different initial points of contact with people with hoarding-like behaviors.

A social worker is often the first professional called in to help someone with hoarding-like behaviors. They may have been called in by the landlord or someone in the apartment complex. The call may have been triggered by an infestation of bugs, smells, or an accumulation of things on the balcony. Sometimes they are brought in by the school because the school is concerned about a child. Teachers notice a child has a rash, is hungry, is dirty (maybe smelly), and thinks the social worker should pay a visit to the home. The job of the social worker is to assess the home situation and develop goals and strategies to improve the well-being of the family. They will also help the family receive support and connect them with various resources. They focus on health and safety concerns for the family. As a professional, they remain nonjudgmental.

Perhaps the person has visited a psychologist or psychiatrist first. Very likely the person initiated the visit for help with another issue like depression or ADHD. As sessions continue, the hoarding-like behaviors may surface. These trained professionals can often get to the root of what caused the original hoard and make recommendations. Most psychologists or psychiatrists do not visit homes. However, they may send an intern to the home to make an assessment. Some doctors prefer to have the person talk about the contents of their home through pictures. They may also refer the person to a professional organizer trained in working with people with hoarding-like behaviors.

The organizer must recognize the courage it takes for someone with hoarding-like behaviors to reach out for help.

Sometimes it is the professional organizer who is the first to arrive. They may have been contacted by a relative or possibly by the person themselves. The organizer may enter the home to find themselves over their head (maybe even literally) with this potential client. They may realize right away that this job is not for them. The role of the professional organizer is to improve the organization of the home. If they realize that the situation is outside their area of expertise, the best thing they can do is exit gracefully.

This has happened to Jonda. Another organizer (Sheila) found herself working with someone and she knew she was making no progress. Sheila was honest with the client and asked if she had her permission to bring another organizer on board. Sheila called Jonda. The two organizers worked together with the client for a couple of sessions, until the client was comfortable with the new situation. In every case, the organizer must recognize the courage it takes for someone with hoarding-like behaviors to reach out for help. It is the organizer's responsibility to see that the client gets the best help available.

Occasionally, it is a first responder who enters the home first. They may have been called for a medical emergency or a fire. While they will not work with the person to clear the hoard, they do need to know how to react when they encounter the hoarded home.

Take Care of Yourself Physically

Working with a person with hoarding-like behaviors is not for the timid or weak of heart. There are a lot of challenges. Those first service providers or even first responders must take care of themselves if they are going to help the individual. They may be blindsided on the first visit and not be prepared to actually start work because the home is much more hoarded than they imagined. They may not either be wearing the right clothes and/or have the right supplies.

Hoarding situations can be unsafe. In some cases, the home is infested with bugs, vermin, critters, mold or mildew. Some providers develop long-term medical symptoms from working in a hoarded environment because they worked too many hours in a home where there was significant mold or mildew.

The home may also have structural problems. There may be so much stuff piled that the floor is in jeopardy of caving in. Jonda worked in a home where the homeowner told her not to get too close to the refrigerator because the floor was giving way. In another home, the banister on the stairs was loose because the homeowner had to climb up the pile of stuff cluttering the stairs while hanging onto the banister.

Because you may be working in an area where you may not even see the floor, wear shoes that are solid; no sandals or open-toed shoes. There might be a bug infestation so wear socks that cover your ankles. Bring bug spray. Diane puts on the bug spray before leaving her home so that she will not embarrass the client. Wear a shirt with long sleeves that you can button and turn up the collar. Wear a hat so that any spiders or cobwebs don't get caught in your hair. Have a change of clothes in the car so that when you return home, you can strip out of what you're wearing and change before going into your home.

If you are coming into the home to work, bring a bag of essential supplies with you. Have an over-the-door hook so that you can hang the bag on the back of the door. This way, it won't sit on the floor and get mixed in with other items. Have in your bag several types of gloves. Have some disposable ones for keeping your hands dry and protected from unidentified dampness. Have heavier ones to protect yourself from broken glass or needles. Bring masks. Jonda carries a bandana as well as some disposable masks because she has a hard time breathing behind a mask for very long. She believes that she developed a respiratory problem due to working in some environments early on and not wearing a mask. If possible, do not sit down. If you must sit, do not sit on any upholstered furniture. Bugs hide in upholstery!

Stay alert. Keep your eyes, ears, and nose open to signals that there may be dangers that you do not readily see. If you hear rustling noises and there are no pets, there is a likelihood rodents might be living in the walls. A damp, musty smell may indicate mold and mildew. You may notice medication or other indicators that needles may be hidden in the clutter.

If you feel there is a bug or rodent infestation, stop work. Before continuing on this job, make sure an exterminator has taken care of this situation. As part of our agreement, before coming into a home, we ask that any firearms are safely locked away.

Take Care of Yourself Emotionally

Self-care for anyone working in a hoarded home is extremely important. This is challenging work. No matter what happens, you must be patient, even when all that is accomplished in a day is removing one bag of trash.

You may run through many different emotions in the course of a couple of hours. Happiness that your client is tackling the problem; frustration that it's taking so long to go through one pile; more frustration because (in your eyes) it is obviously a pile of trash – so just get rid of it already; anger that so much money has been wasted; distress over the amount of wasted (spoiled) food; empathy for your client because they are really trying.

Allow yourself to feel these negative emotions when you are not with the client. When you are with them, you are their support. You are their cheerleader.

Don't let these negative emotions fester inside you. Express them at home, but be wary of taking out your frustrations with the job on your partner. Take a nice long indulgent shower or bath and wash away these stressful feelings. Compassion fatigue is sometimes hard to recognize. Take care of yourself and give yourself some days off. Set boundaries on how much time each day you work. Be sure to eat well and to get a good night's sleep so that when you return to the job, you will be refreshed and ready to be a patient cheerleader for this person as they start changing their behavior.

While working, keep in mind that this is not your home. Never care more about getting the job done or work harder than the person you are helping. This is easy to say but difficult in practice. It is natural to review and rethink problems into our evenings, trying to come up with better answers. Save the brainstorming for times with the client where they are actively involved in the solutions.

Cleaning Out Never Works

According to the International Obsessive Compulsive Disorder Foundation (link is in the References), cleaning out a hoarded home for someone without their involvement rarely works. This makes perfect sense because when the person doesn't have a say in what stays and what goes, they are inclined to replace those items. Additionally, when therapy is not included in the treatment for the person with hoarding-like behaviors, they are less likely to under-stand the root cause of their collecting and start collecting again.

Diane and Jonda are called by family members from time to time to come in and clean up and organize the mess. This is something neither Diane nor Jonda will do. As we have said in previous chapters, touching someone's belongings without permission is a violation of trust. We always ask that the homeowner give us a call. If they are ready to change their behavior, we will happily work with them to cull their collections and organize their belongings.

Several years ago, Diane was contacted by a young woman to help unpack her mother-in-law (Connie). The story the woman told Diane went like this. She and her husband went to Boston to help pack up Connie's belongings and enough furniture for a two-bedroom condo in Atlanta. The woman wanted to hire Diane to work with Connie to unpack and organize the condo and perhaps provide ongoing monthly maintenance visits because the woman said Connie had a tendency to be messy.

Diane met with Connie and the two worked together to place furniture, unpack boxes, and get the condo set up. As the boxes were unpacked, Diane heard Connie say, "I wish they had let me keep both of these lamps," and "I really liked the other chairs better." She also said things like, "I wish I had a side table to put here. You know, I had lots of little side tables at my other house. They should have put them in the shipment." Diane didn't know how to respond because she didn't know the whole story.

As time went on, Connie told Diane that her son had come to Boston, moved her into a hotel, and cleaned out her home without her input. He and his wife decided for Connie which furniture to bring to Atlanta, which accessories, and which knick-knacks.

Connie was always missing something.

Every time Diane went to Connie's to maintain the organization, she found new things in the condo. After a while, it became apparent that Connie would benefit from therapy. She agreed to see a therapist and that helped a little. But Connie was angry with her son. She felt that although he and his wife had her best interests at heart, they didn't consult her or involve her in the cleaning out process.

Consequently, her home, her new condo in Atlanta, became filled up and overflowing with stuff just like her home in Boston had been.

Cleaning out a hoarded home doesn't solve the problem.

Acquaint Yourself with Some Do's and Don'ts

When you are starting your journey with this person with hoarding-like behaviors, keep an open mind. Listen to everything they say and notice their tone of voice and body language. Realize that it took a lot of courage for them to reach out to you and agree to start work. Consider the possibility that this might not even be a hoarding situation. Acquaint yourself with the definition of hoarding. As you listen to their story, consider that this might be a temporary situational problem or perhaps they have always had a hard time getting organized. Ask yourself these questions: Have they moved recently? Has there been a death in the family? Has there been a change in health? Has there been a job change, a change in routines?

Never assume that you know what is going on. Never judge the person by what you see first or by what others have told you.

When you start working on clearing the space, start small. With time, small steps will lead to big results. If you come into an area that distresses the person, ask questions to lead them into telling you more. If it's too upsetting, offer to leave this area and move to another space.

In Conclusion

We have focused on some of the worst possible scenarios so that as a professional, you are prepared for anything. Most of the time, the situations will not be this challenging. Remain calm and gentle with the people you work with and with yourself. If you find yourself in a situation that is more that you can handle, do your absolute best to find some other support for the person or for yourself. Also be aware that there are times when nothing you or anyone else does is going to change the situation. Once you have done your best to make the home safe, you are through. Some people will prefer to continue to live with this lifestyle.

CHAPTER 9

Living & Staying Safe Within This Lifestyle

As much as you want to help someone with hoarding-like behaviors, if they are not ready and open to receiving help, there is only so much you can do. The person may have many reasons not to change at this time. If they live alone, they may argue that their clutter is not hurting anyone and that their belongings bring them pleasure. Perhaps even the acquiring of new things is one of their few real pleasures. Intellectually, they probably know that they should tidy up. At the very least, they privately acknowledge this is not the best way to live. If they tell you they are perfectly happy the way things are, you must accept that.

Acknowledge that the person has the right to make their own decisions. It is important to remember that this is not about the "stuff." It is more about the value they place on the objects, even if you do not see them as useful.

Instead of looking for ways to remove the hoard, look for ways to help the person remain safe in their home. Provide a supportive environment that encourages the person to eventually seek some help. Remembering that even accepting that there is a problem is their decision alone. Listen with an open mind and offer information when appropriate. Let them know that you are only concerned for their health, safety, and happiness.

Health

There are so many things that can cause poor health in a filled up or hoarded home. When routine household maintenance tasks go unattended, mold and mildew appear in random places. When excess dust accumulates, it contributes to poor air quality, particularly if the windows are tightly shut and air vents are blocked. Then there's also the possibility of consuming spoiled food which has lingered too long in the refrigerator. These maintenance details can cause health problems.

We are bringing these things to your attention here because if you're allowed in the home, dealing with these issues may help you start reducing the hoard. You can tell the person you want to help that you are concerned for their health.

Air circulation, poor ventilation, and the accumulation of carbon dioxide is something that is relatively easy to fix. As we said, windows are generally kept tightly shut in a hoarded home. Quite often, boxes and other things are stacked in front of the windows and around the perimeter of the room which limits access to the windows.

Air vents are also found near the perimeter of the room. If things are stacked on top of vents and the windows are tightly shut, there is a strong possibility that the air circulation in this room, and possibly the rest of the home, is not adequate.

During a conversation with your friend or family member, you might casually say, "It's a little stuffy in here. Do you think so too? Or is it just me?" You continue by telling the person that a while ago you noticed the air in your living room was feeling stuffy. Then you noticed that, by mistake, someone had put something on top of a couple of the air vents in front of a window. As soon as you moved those things and opened the window, the air flow was better in your living room. You were so happy to have solved the problem. Because you're talking about something in YOUR home and not pointing a finger at them, they may walk away thinking that maybe they have some things stacked on top of the vents or in front of a window.

Casual conversations are wonderful ways to talk about topics that may be sensitive.

We find that casual conversations are wonderful ways to talk about topics that may be sensitive. You can bring up the fact that regularly wiping up moisture helps to prevent mold and mildew from growing near the kitchen faucet. The more mold and mildew are kept at bay, the better the air quality. The less likelihood to develop respiratory infections.

It may happen that the homeowner needs to have a plumber come in to fix a leaky kitchen or bathroom faucet, to fix a toilet that is running, or to repair a leaking pipe under a sink. This need gives you an opportunity to talk about how helpful the plumber you used was and to let the person know the plumber gave you some handy tips for preventing mold in your bathroom. You can provide the name of a plumber you used when requested.

If you know that the person has allergies, you can address the topic of dust, mold, mildew, and air quality from the position that you absolutely know they will feel better, be less affected by recurring illness due to their allergies, when the air can circulate better through the house and when mold and mildew are kept to a minimum.

Continually beating the person over the head, telling them they are living in an unhealthy environment will only push them away. You know, they've told you, they are fine with their living situation. Offer them tiny tips from time to time.

If they have an interest in a particular charity, let them know when that organization is collecting books and magazines. Tell them that you are going on Tuesday next week to deliver your books and magazines and that you'd be happy to bring their donation or simply to have their company. This may prompt them to do some decluttering.

When and if you're permitted to be inside the house and allowed to help, offer to do small tasks.

A possible scenario could involve helping to put groceries away. Ask if it would be alright to put the non-perishable things away in the pantry. Then ask if you can group categories of cans together. If possible, put the older cans to the front of the shelf and the newer ones behind. Casually look at the cans and comment, saying something like," I noticed this can is rusty. May I toss it in the trash?" Chances are, you'll be able to toss a couple of things if you approach the topic sensitively. Anything you can clear away reduces the possibility that the person will get food poisoning.

Picking up trash in the house, in particular food wrappers or old take-out containers, will help to discourage mice and other rodents or cockroaches from coming in. Be careful in your approach. You know that if you're too aggressive in cleaning up, you will not be allowed back in.

As you're standing in the room, if there happens to be something at your feet, ask if you can pick it up for the person. You don't need to make a big deal out of it and you don't need to go looking for other things to throw away. Just ask about the one or two small things that are right by you and are obviously trash.

Be observant but try not to be obvious about it. You may notice that lots of trash lands on the floor near the recliner. Ask if you can put a trash can next to the recliner. The person may be inclined to put the trash in the trash can if it's convenient to use.

If you know the person has a bad shoulder and has a hard time reaching up for things, you can offer to help by saying you know it's difficult to reach these high shelves. In fact, that may be an opportunity for you to do a small amount of reorganizing, making it easier for the person to get a hold of the things they need. You may be able to put things up high they don't need to access often and clear a table top or a counter for the things they use all the time.

Safety

Safety within a hoarded home is another big issue. When stacks of things grow too tall, they can topple over. If the homeowner wants something in the middle of the stack, they may get impatient and undo the stack, leaving the contents strewn about the floor. Things are often left lying about for a variety of reasons. It may be because the home is so full that there's no place to put them, the person doesn't know where to put them, or because they were so intent on the object in their hands that they forgot to pick up the pile.

Clutter can cause trip hazards. When these things are left lying about in random places, the person could trip, fall, and possibly be seriously injured.

Talk to the person living in the home about having pathways from the front door to the back door and emphasize the necessity of being able to easily open those doors. By easily, we mean the doors can open all the way or, at the very least, wide enough to let a gurney through.

Mention that if there was a medical emergency, the person would want the first responders to be able to come through the door with a gurney. These same first responders need to be able to get through the home unimpeded.

If, by chance, there are things that are cluttering the hallways and the floor or blocking the doors, this may be your opportunity to ask – for medical safety reasons – if you could make those areas safe. Explain that you would create stable piles and that you would only throw something out with permission.

Ask if you have permission to throw out old and empty take-out containers, empty food wrappers, used napkins, paper towels, and tissues. Use a clear garbage bag so the person can easily see that you are only throwing out things from this list. Explain that (as we mentioned previously) these things attract mice and other rodents.

These critters will sometimes chew on electrical wires. Frayed wires can cause a short in the system and an electrical fire. You want the person to be safe in their home. One way to ensure their safety is to prevent a fire by removing trash and limiting the possibility that critters will want to come in.

If papers are being stacked on top of the stove or stored inside the oven, suggest another place to keep these things. Since paper is combustible, it is important that it's not stored or stacked anywhere near the oven or stovetop. Ask to move those papers to the dining table or family room. You may end up piling papers on top of existing piles, but that is better than leaving the papers in the kitchen.

Another place to keep clear off random bits of stuff is the furnace. Having piles of things around or near the furnace is also a fire hazard.

The person you're helping will understand but may be reluctant to have you do anything about the magnitude of things lying around. It may simply be overwhelming.

We suggest that you ask if you have permission to make small changes. Tackle the obvious fire hazards first – things on the stove top or in the oven. Then talk about removing things from around the furnace. As you work, ask if you can make small, stable piles wherever you are in the home to minimize tripping hazards.

Small changes lead to big changes. Do not attempt big changes at first or you will be asked to leave.

Small changes lead to big changes.

Happiness

Experience with our clients tells us that shopping and bringing something new (even bringing something old but new to the person) into the home gives a person with hoarding-like behaviors a euphoric feeling. We all know that feeling. The problem is, that feeling doesn't last.

Another problem is that generally speaking, people who fill their homes to the point of being full want their homes to be that way. They are not happy or comfortable with clear counters or table-tops. They want to be cocooned inside their homes. They want the walls of things.

Urging someone to clear these spaces all at once is not productive. Instead, aim to reduce the height of the walls or the bulk of the things on the counters or tabletops.

Happiness is a subjective emotion. What makes you happy may not make someone else happy. In fact, a clear table with a vase of flowers may make you happy but may cause someone else to be anxious or stressed. Let the person with whom you are working tell you what makes them happy.

Think back to our client whose car was full of school supplies she bought to give to elementary school children. Acquiring these things and visualizing donating these school supplies brought our client happiness.

Having a conversation about what makes the person happy will help to determine if donating some portion of the accumulated things to an organization the person likes will bring them joy. Maybe they will be able to substitute the happy feeling they get in acquiring things with the happy feeling of making someone else happy by shopping from their home.

While it's difficult to get a person to stop acquiring, if you can get them to release some of their belongings to organizations they believe in, they may begin to reduce the amount of stuff in their home.

For instance, if they have an abundance of wool, they may feel good about donating some of the wool to a group of knitters who make caps for newborn babies. If they have a collection of old towels, sheets, or blankets, they may be inclined to give some to an animal shelter. Make a date and take the person to the organization so they can see for themselves how happy the donation of their belongings makes the recipients feel.

As you talk with the person you are helping, listen for clues as to the organizations that they may want to help. There are so many needy groups. Find some in your community with which your friend or family member can connect.

Maintenance

We are not talking about true organizing maintenance here. We are talking about you maintaining your relationship with your friend or family member. We suggest you schedule regular times to check back in with them. They will begin to expect you and most likely look forward to your visits.

As you visit, check to see if it's necessary to restack a pile or provide better access to a door. Of course, you will only do these things with the person's permission.

Above all else, the very most important thing you can do is to be there for them. You may be their lifeline to the outside world, as you are probably the only one allowed in. Maintain the trust they place in you.

In Conclusion

While you may be convinced that you know what is best, right or good for a friend or loved one living in a hoarded home, in order to keep them healthy, happy and safe, you are not the decision maker. What makes you feel happy or safe may not be what works for them. Ultimately, if you are allowed to come in, make suggestions, make a few small changes, accept that as good enough. If the time ever comes that they are no longer willing to have you in their home, walk away knowing in your heart that you did everything in your power to help this person make positive changes in their environment.

EPILOGUE

Between the two of us we have more than 30 years of experience working with clients affected by chronic disorganization and hoarding. Many of our clients are also affected by other medically diagnosed disorders. We treasure the time we have spent with each and every client. We learn something new during almost every organizing session. Perhaps it's a new way to do a familiar task or a different way to use an everyday item. Why? Because each person is different. Each person brings their unique way of being and doing to the organizing process. That's what keeps us coming back for more. There's nothing routine about our business.

This book is our love letter to our clients. We thank them all, from the bottom of our hearts, for the trust and faith they put in us. We thank them for allowing us to be part of their organizing journey.

APPENDIX: REFERENCES & RESOURCES

Chapter 2

Wikipedia article on the history of surnames.
https://en.wikipedia.org/wiki/Surname

The Journal of Personality and Social Psychology: an article on Self-talk http://selfcontrol.psych.lsa.umich.edu/wp-content/uploads/2014/01/KrossJ_Pers_Soc_Psychol2014Self-talk_as_a_regulatory_mechanism_How_you_do_it_matters.pdf

American Psychiatric Association: What is Hoarding? https://www.psychiatry.org/patients-families/hoarding-disorder/what-is-hoarding-disorder

Chapter 5

A study on the emotional/psychological impact of hoarding clean-outs on clients: https://www.therecoveryvillage.com/mental-health/hoarding/related/how-to-stage-hoarding-intervention/

Chapter 8

The International Obsessive Compulsive Disorder Foundation article on cleaning out a hoarded home: https://hoarding.iocdf.org/for-families/how-to-help-a-loved one-with-hd/

Books

Beattie, Jonda. *From Vision to Victory: A Workbook For Finding a Simple Path to an Organized Home* 2009 Decatur, GA. Squall Press

Birchall, Elaine, Suzanne Cronkwright *Conquer the Clutter; Strategies to Identify, Manage, and Overcome Hoarding* 2019 Baltimore, MD Johns Hopkins University Press

Bratiotis, Christiana, Cristina Sorrentino Schmalisch, and Gail Steketee *The Hoarding Handbook; A Guide for Human Service Professionals* 2011 New York, NY Oxford University Press

Dellaquila, Vickie. *Don't Toss My Memories in the Trash; A Step-by-Step Guide to Helping Seniors Downsize, Organize, and* Move 2007 USA Mountain Publishing

Frost, Randy O., Gail Steketee *STUFF; Compulsive Hoarding and the Meaning of Things* 2010 Boston, MA Houghton Mifflin Harcourt

Kolberg, Judith and Kathleen Nadeau. *ADD-Friendly Ways to Organize Your Life* Second Edition 2017 New York, NY. Routledge

Kolberg, Judith. *What Every Professional Organizer Needs to Know About Hoarding* Second Edition 2009 Decatur, GA *Squall* Press

Neziroglu, Fugen, Jerome Bubrick, Jose A. Yaryura-Tobias *Overcoming Compulsive Hoarding* 2004 Oakland, CA New Harbinger Publications, Inc.

Sgro, Valentina *Heart of a Hoarder* 2008 Cleveland, OH Green Square Publishing

Spetalnik, Maria *Hoarding for Law Enforcement and other Public Officials* 2016

Thomas, Geralin *From Hoarding to Hope Understanding People Who Hoard and How to Help Them* 2015 Cary, NC. MetroZing Publishing

Tolin, David F., Randy O. Frost, Gail Steketee *Buried in Treasures Help for Compulsive Acquiring, Saving, and Hoarding* 2007 New York, NY Oxford University Press

Tompkins, Michael A., Tamara L. Hartl *Digging Out Helping Your Loved One Manage Clutter, Hoarding & Compulsive Acquiring* 2009 Oakland, CA New Harbinger Publications, Inc.

Chapter 1: Useful Tools

Clutter-Hoarding Scale® was developed by the Institute for Challenging Disorganization. It is a 16-page document that can be downloaded from the ICD website. The Clutter–Hoarding Scale® is an assessment measurement tool, which gives professional organizers and related professionals definitive parameters related to health and safety. https://www.challengingdisorganization.org/clutter-hoarding-scale

Clutter Image Rating Scale was developed by Dr. Randy Frost and the International Obsessive Compulsive Disorder Foundation. This rating scale uses a series of 9 pictures of different rooms in a home filled with clutter at varying levels. A person challenged by clutter can point to the picture that best represents the level of clutter in their kitchen, bedroom, living room and other rooms typically found in a home. Download the Clutter Image Rating scale from this link: https://hoarding.iocdf.org/wp-content/uploads/sites/7/2016/12/Clutter-Image-Rating-3-18-16.pdf

Clutter Quality of Life Scale was developed by Dr. Catherine Roster and the Institute for Challenging Disorganization® (ICD). This scale asks a person to answer questions which reveal the impact clutter is having on their quality of life, specifically on their relationships, finances, work and home life. It is available on the ICD website: www.challengingdisorganization.org

The DSM-5 Diagnostic Criteria for Hoarding

1. Persistent difficulty or parting with possessions, regardless of their actual value.

2. This difficulty is due to a perceived need to save the items and to distress associated with discarding them.

3. The difficulty discarding possessions results in the accumulation of possessions that congest and clutter active living areas and substantially compromises their intended use. If living areas are uncluttered, it is only because of the interventions of third parties (e.g., family members, cleaners, authorities).

4. The hoarding causes clinically significant distress or impairment in social, occupational or other important areas of functioning (including maintaining a safe environment for self and others).

5. The hoarding is not attributable to another medical condition (e.g., brain injury, cerebrovascular disease, Prader-Willi syndrome).

6. The hoarding is not better explained by the symptoms of another mental disorder (e.g., obsessions in obsessive-compulsive disorder, delusions in schizophrenia or another psychotic disorder, cognitive deficits in major neurocognitive disorder, restricted interests in autism spectrum disorder).

The hoarder engages in excessive acquisition, buys items that are unnecessary and they do not have space for. The hoarder may have good insight and realize that their hoarding is a problem or have poor insight and not recognize their behavior is unhealthy.

According to the DSM-5, 80-90% of hoarders also engage in excessive shopping and buying unnecessary items.

DSM-5 also reports that 2% to 6% of the population have a Hoarding Disorder. Although hoarding is more common in older adults (55-94 years), it appears to begin at 11-15 years, and starts to cause significant impairment when people are in their 30s. Hoarding is no longer considered a type of obsessive-compulsive disorder (OCD); but 20 percent of people with Hoarding Disorder also have OCD and are likely to collect strange objects like trash, feces, urine, nails, hair and rotten food.

Taken from: https://www.theravive.com/therapedia/hoarding-disorder-dsm--5-300.3-(f42)

Chapter 7: List of Supplies to Have on Hand

1. Over-the-door hook (for your tote bag, lunch bag, tools and more)

2. Clear trash bags

3. Disposable gloves

4. Heavy gloves

5. Face mask

6. Boxes for sorting

7. Tape

8. Marking pens

9. Post-It Notes®

10. Hand sanitizer

Professional Organizers

If you are struggling with clutter in a filled up home or know someone who does, you will want to hire someone with education regarding the Hoarding Disorder and chronic disorganization. Please take time to look at the professional's credentials.

These two links will help you locate a professional organizer in your area.

The Institute for Challenging Disorganization: www.challenging-disorganization.org

The National Association for Productivity and Organizing Professionals: www.napo.net

Hoarding-Related Websites

If you or someone you know has hoarding-like behavior, please refer to any of these websites:

www.childrenofhoarders.com

www.clutterersanonymous.org

https://hoarding.iocdf.org/for-families/how-to-help-a-loved one-with-hd/

https://messies.com/

www.squalorsurvivors.com

Acknowledgments

We started working on this book shortly after giving a presentation to our NAPO-Georgia professional organizing colleagues in November 2018. Julie Bestry came up to us and said, "You have a book here. Why don't you turn this into a book? It would be great!"

We thought about it – sort of.

Then a few months later, Diane took a writer's workshop course with Melanie Gorman from YourTango. Towards the end of one of the classes, Melanie told the group that she often works with authors to create their book proposal. The light bulb went on in Diane's head. She asked Jonda if she would be interested in looking into this. The rest is history. Melanie has faithfully guided us through the process of writing this fabulous book. She helped us merge and meld our distinct writing styles to create this book. We are forever thankful.

Melanie also introduced us to Jennifer S. Wilkov of Your Book is Your Hook, LLC. Jennifer is a master at getting people to express their true vision or mission for their business. Through Jennifer's thoughtful guidance we have created not only this book but also a new business platform and several related products. Jennifer is truly gifted. She pushed us to think quite a bit outside the box. We are forever thankful to her also.

A big thank you also to Diane's cousin, Vanessa Robisch, and Diane's sister-in-law, Joan Norfleet, for reading and editing our manuscript. After a while, many of the pages were somewhat memorized. We could no more have spotted a word out of place than we could have flown to the moon. Thank you both very much.

Stay Connected

To continue to receive information from Diane and Jonda about *Filled Up and Overflowing* and much more, follow Release•Repurpose•Reorganize at:

Twitter

Jonda = @timespaceorg

Diane = @DianeNQuintana

Facebook

www.facebook.com/Ask-the-Organizers-Diane-and-Jonda

Instagram

Jonda = @jondabeattie

Diane = @dnq_solutions

Pinterest

www.pinterest.com/ReleaseRepurposeReorganize

LinkedIn

www.linkedin.com/company/release-repurpose-reorganize-llc/

YouTube

https://youtube.com/user/jondabeattie

Follow our **BLOG** at www.ReleaseRepurpose.com where you can find more articles and tips about hoarding-like behaviors and how to clear your space so you can create your place of refuge.

Sign up for our **NEWSLETTER** at www.ReleaseRepurpose.com to keep up to date with our latest techniques.

We Speak!

Hire us to speak for your group, office, or organization or attend our workshops to learn more about:

- Organize Don't Traumatize

- Paper Organizing Challenges

- Plan to Lose

- Downsizing? The What, Why, and How

- De-Clutter to De-Stress

- The 411 on Hoarding

- Surviving the Holidaze

> Don't see a topic you have in mind? Contact us at www.ReleaseRepurpose.com. We are happy to put together the perfect presentation for you.

Join us for an upcoming workshop!

Not sure you need us for a big job but interested in working with us during a workshop? We'd love to help you with these events:

- Paper Piles to Files – *bring us a paper bag filled with paper and we will help you turn it into organized files.*

- Surviving the Holidaze – *Come with your calendar and ideas of things you want to do, make, and experience during/throughout the holidays; leave with a step-by-step guide to make it all happen in the ways you imagined it.*

Sign up at www.ReleaseRepurpose.com for our upcoming workshops!

Services

Feeling overwhelmed by the amount of stuff in your home?

Not sure where to begin or how to clear the space for you?

Join our clutter support group

Clear Space for You is our online virtual clutter support group which is limited to four people. This is a semi-private safe space where you can get all your questions answered. This group meets weekly.

Visit our website for more information: https://releaserepurpose. com/clutter-support-group/

Want to work with us privately?

We offer one-on-one virtual support sessions.

For more information:

https://releaserepurpose.com/clutter-support-group-2/

About the Authors

Diane N. Quintana is a Certified Professional Organizer and owner of DNQ Solutions, LLC, based in Atlanta, Georgia. A seasoned expert in her field, Diane led the organizing team for an episode of A&E "Hoarders" show in 2011 and provided several after-care organizing sessions for the segment participant. She has been featured in *Real Simple* magazine and has appeared on the Atlanta "Friends and Neighbors" show.

An accomplished speaker and author of four books including *Flying Solo: A Guide to Organizing Your Home When You Leave Your Parents' Nest* and *Now What? A Simple Organizing Guide,* Diane most recently co-authored the illustrated children's books *Suzie's Messy Room* and *Benji's Messy Room* with Jonda Beattie.

As a mother and former elementary school teacher, Diane has lived and worked in four countries including Asia and the United States.

Diane teaches professionals, men and women and working mothers, how to become organized and provides them with strategies and solutions for maintaining order in their busy lives. She specializes in residential and home-office organizing in metropolitan Atlanta and in working with people affected by ADD, Hoarding, and Chronic Disorganization.

Diane is a member of the Institute for Challenging Disorganization (ICD), The National Association of Productivity and Organizing Professionals (NAPO), and NAPO-Georgia. She is certified in Chronic Disorganization through the ICD, holds Hoarding and Attention Deficit Disorder specialist certificates, and is a Master Trainer. Diane is also a consultant with Parkaire Consultants in Atlanta.

Jonda S. Beattie is a Professional Organizer, presenter, and author of several books on organization for kids and adults. Notably, Jonda cut her teeth in the television market, appearing as part of the organizational team for both "Hoarding" (A&E Network, 2011) and "Buried Alive" (TLC Network, 2009). She has also been interviewed about organizational challenges on PBS' "Friends and Neighbors" Show, Fox 5 "Good Day Atlanta," and on "Book Your Success" (local Atlanta television program).

Jonda is the author of an organizational workbook, *From Vision to Victory: A Workbook For Finding a Simple Path to an Organized Home*. She has also co-authored two children's books, *Suzie's Messy Room* and *Benji's Messy Room*, named lovingly after her second son, Benjamin. Her work has been featured in *Women's World* magazine, and she has contributed several times to *Getting Organized Magazine* in the Ask the Experts section. Jonda writes a weekly blog for the past 11 years sharing her insights with clients and readers about organizing every aspect of your life, from parties to death and everything in between.

Professionally, Jonda is a member of CHADD (Children and Adults with Attention-Deficit/Hyperactivity Disorder) and an active member of NAPO (National Association of Productivity & Organizing Professionals) both nationally and locally. She is also a member of ICD (Institute for Challenging Disorganization) where she has Level 1 Certificates in Chronic Disorganization and Basic Hoarding. She has taken over 20 classes on Hoarding and teaches classes on Organizing Paperwork for the Special Needs Child.

In her spare time, Jonda enjoys traveling, cooking, and giving parties or simply sitting on the deck enjoying the birds.

About Diane and Jonda

Diane and Jonda are both former elementary school teachers. They met while doing volunteer work for NAPO (the National Association of Productivity and Organizing Specialists; www.napo.net) at a local elementary school in Atlanta.

When Diane was faced with a particularly challenging organizing situation in a hoarded home, she called Jonda to work with her. They realized that since they were both trained special education teachers, they had a similar approach to helping people affected by hoarding-like behaviors and chronic disorganization - an approach unlike any of their colleagues.

Together they worked on the Atlanta Hoarding Task Force under the direction of Judith Kolberg. Judith is the founder of the National Study Group on Chronic Disorganization, which has since become The Institute for Challenging Disorganization. This task force was aligned with a junk removal company as well as a bio-hazard cleaning group. After several years of trying to secure funding and status as a 501C3, the group was disbanded.

This early start in working with people affected by the Hoarding Disorder and hoarding-like behaviors inspired Diane and Jonda with their shared appreciation for the challenges people face when attempting to reduce the amount of stuff in their homes.

Diane and Jonda each run their own organizing businesses. They chose to create a business together because they realized their mission and focus was similar and that they would make an even bigger impact by combining their efforts. They continue to love giving workshops and presentations together. Now they offer virtual support groups as well as individual virtual support for people who feel overwhelmed by clutter.

Made in the USA
Las Vegas, NV
03 February 2021